Many-Sided Wisdom

A New Politics of the Spirit

First published by O Books, 2010
O Books is an imprint of John Hunt Publishing Ltd., The Bothy, Deershot Lodge, Park Lane, Ropley,
Hants, SO24 0BE, UK
office1@o-books.net
www.o-books.net

Distribution in:	South Africa
	Stephan Phillips (pty) Ltd
UK and Europe	Email: orders@stephanphillips.com
Orca Book Services	Tel: 27 21 4489839 Telefax: 27 21 4479879
orders@orcabookservices.co.uk	
Tel: 01202 665432 Fax: 01202 666219	Text copyright Aidan Rankin 2008
Int. code (44)	
	Design: Stuart Davies
USA and Canada	
NBN	ISBN: 978 1 84694 277 8
custserv@nbnbooks.com	
Tel: 1 800 462 6420 Fax: 1 800 338 4550	All rights reserved. Except for brief quotations
	in critical articles or reviews, no part of this
Australia and New Zealand	book may be reproduced in any manner without
Brumby Books	prior written permission from the publishers.
sales@brumbybooks.com.au	
Tel: 61 3 9761 5535 Fax: 61 3 9761 7095	The rights of Aidan Rankin as author have been
	asserted in accordance with the Copyright,
Far East (offices in Singapore, Thailand,	Designs and Patents Act 1988.
Hong Kong, Taiwan)	
Pansing Distribution Pte Ltd	
kemal@pansing.com	A CIP catalogue record for this book is available
Tel: 65 6319 9939 Fax: 65 6462 5761	from the British Library.

Printed by Digital Book Print

O Books operates a distinctive and ethical publishing philosophy in
all areas of its business, from its global network of authors to
production and worldwide distribution.

Many-Sided Wisdom

A New Politics of the Spirit

Aidan Rankin

BOOKS

Winchester, UK
Washington, USA

CONTENTS

Don't fight darkness. Bring the light and the darkness will disappear.
Maharishi Mahesh Yogi, 2006

To my mother and father,
Anne and David Rankin,
with love and gratitude

Foreword

By Paul de Leeuw MA, *Kannushi* (Shinto Master)

Although this is the first time I have heard the word *Anekant* – and perhaps I am not the only one – its meaning and the idea behind it, Many-Sidedness, are by no means unfamiliar to me. I therefore felt honored when Dr Aidan Rankin asked me to write a foreword to his new book and it is with great pleasure that I accept his invitation.

More than thirty years ago I learned for the first time about the existence of something similar to the Indic (and specifically Jain) concept of Anekant. This was an exciting discovery and its transformative potential – both for the individual and society – struck an immediate chord with me. The setting was another Asian country, Japan, and the man who revealed to me the existence of Many-Sidedness was Dr Jean Herbert, the French diplomat and philosopher.

In the twentieth century, Herbert was the first western researcher to investigate seriously the various aspects of Shinto in Japan. He visited many and varied shrines and interviewed many eminent persons who served at the shrines as Masters (*kannushi*) or Grand Masters (*guji*) of Shinto. This was in preparation for his book, which is still the definitive work on Shinto outside of Japan, where it is also revered. On reading his notes, Herbert found striking discontinuities between the statements of his informants. Often, what they said was contradictory and rarely did their definitions of Shinto concur. This led him to the initial conclusion that Shinto, unlike most other world religions, did not possess a coherent body of doctrine or 'core' beliefs.

To determine 'the truth', Herbert organized a conference at which the wide range of Shinto Masters and adepts who had contributed to his research were confronted with each other's contradictory statements. The proceedings of this meeting left him, as he told me, 'speechless'. Instead of discussing the rights and wrongs of each statement, each delegate opted for a peaceful coexistence by acknowledging: 'My truth does not need to be the same as yours.'

In the west, we are still strongly conditioned by the idea that Aidan Rankin calls 'either/or' logic. This stipulates that everything is either 'A' or 'not-A'. The sense that it is possible to be two (or more) 'things' at once remains somewhat alien, despite the conclusions of modern science which point us increasingly towards a Many-Sided view of the universe. In the area of political and economic ideology, either/or logic – or One-Sidedness – remains entrenched. It is the adversarial approach to politics – rather than the details of the political ideologies themselves – that is the true cause of conflict and violence. And violence, as Rankin points out, can be intellectual and dialectical as much as physical. Indeed thoughts guided by hatred, intolerance and One-Sidedness are *in themselves* acts of violence that lead directly to psychic and physical harm, including dictatorship, terrorism and war. As the great Prussian military tactician Carl von Clausewitz concluded in the 1820s: 'war is merely the continuation of politics'. This is why Anekant – Many-Sidedness – involves a reconditioning of the mind and a change in the way we approach ideas and thoughts.

Jean Herbert realized that when approaching Shinto he was experiencing a clash of cultural assumptions. Put simply, a western culture of either/or was coming face to face with an Asian culture of both/and. From this experience, he concluded that Shinto is like a river, from which everybody may take the water he or she needs. And this inspired the title of his book, *Shinto: At the Fountainhead of Japan*, the English edition of which was published in 1967. To Shinto practitioners, life is also like a river and we take from it what we need, not more, not less and not otherwise. This idea, at once simple and complex, corresponds with the Jain idea of Anekant. It can also be said that Dr Herbert's conclusions about Shinto are a working example of Many-Sidedness. They are based on respect for diversity and an acceptance that beneath the difference of opinion or practice there is the same truth.

Before he came to Shinto, Jean Herbert extensively studied Buddhist and Hindu philosophies – from the Indic tradition of which Jainism is also an integral part. He was aware of their flexibility, tolerance and quiet strength, and believed before it was fashionable that these teachings had much to offer the west. In addition to his distinguished academic career, he was also a pioneering worker on behalf of the League of Nations and later the United Nations, as well as the International Labour Office and other trans-national bodies. He published the definitive *Interpreter's Handbook* in 1952. These apparently varied aspects of his career in fact come together like pieces in a jigsaw puzzle. International bodies are – or at least should be – about finding common ground despite cultural and ideological differences. Interpreting is not translation in the literal sense. Often, it is less about rendering words exactly from one language to another and more about conveying nuance and attitude to those who speak and think differently.

Shinto, the Way of the Kami, is inherently pluralist. The *kami*, of which there are many thousands, are not simply 'gods' or 'deities' in the way these terms have been understood in the west and near east since antiquity. They can exercise divine power, but they are better understood as archetypes, or expressions of forces within nature and the cosmos – and within ourselves. We can identify with whichever kami best suit our disposition, circumstances and spiritual needs. The kami are therefore Many-Sided. Jainism is a non-theistic religion, whose exemplars are the 'Path-Finders': exceptional human beings who eventually achieve enlightenment. However at a certain level both faiths arrive at remarkably similar conclusions about the Many-Sided nature of reality and truth.

What is more, this view of life enables us to renew our relationship with nature. We can see that we are part of it, not apart from it, and that human welfare depends on working with the natural world, not against it. It is in this search for renewal that Dr Rankin and I have met. I totally agree with his statement at the end of this book: 'The sense that we are in conflict with our environment, and need to reconnect with it, coincides with a revival of nature-centered spiritualities, from Shinto in Japan to African traditional religions, [which invoke] the natural forces of the universe.' The truth remains the same, whether we express it through the language and imagery of Shinto, Jainism, Christianity or any spiritual path, whether chosen or inherited.

Through his exploration of Anekant, Dr Rankin is continuing and building upon the tradition of Jean Herbert. Like Herbert, Rankin seeks after the perennial wisdom that is the origin and the conclusion of all spiritual inquiry. He holds up to the light a Many-Sided spiritual jewel, but also shows us that Anekant can provide a practical guide for living in the modern world.

Two years ago, Aidan Rankin and I joined forces in the editing of a western version of a Japanese book, *The Essence of Shinto: Japan's Spiritual Heart*. During the process of our co-operation we were aware of the difference between what can broadly be described as 'eastern' and 'western' attitudes to the relationship between humanity and nature. Whereas the eastern impulse was towards integration, the western impulse was towards compartmentalization and separation. However, the social and economic division between humankind and nature needs to be bridged if we are to approach our environment in an intelligent and enlightened manner.

Ancient traditions like Jainism and Shinto are therefore more relevant than ever to the modern world. For more than thirty years I have studied and practiced the ancient Japanese tradition of Shinto. In the beginning this was not easy, partly due to the common opinion that Shinto cannot be understood by a non-Japanese person. Thanks to the generosity of a more universally minded Japanese Grand Master, I was able to enter his Shinto school. Eventually, I became the first non-Japanese person to receive a license as a Shinto Master (*kannushi*) in order to perform Shinto ceremonies. These ceremonies transmit ancient and unwritten knowledge about how to connect with nature. Jainism also, as one of the earliest sources of Indic wisdom, makes the most ancient forms of spiritual wisdom resonate with modern men and women.

In one of the esoteric techniques of Shinto, the student learns to explore his or her inner self. The aim is to find the spiritual centre of that self and through that the point of origin of the universe. Upon arrival at the center of the cosmos, the student becomes aware of a universal 'viewpoint', in which the many apparently incompatible or contradictory perspectives discover a Many-Sided unity. This experience of transformation is essentially the same as the Jain technique of Anekant. Anekant is derived from Jain teachings, but as Dr Rankin shows, it has universal significance.

I am more than happy that Dr Rankin has explored and explained the Jain tradition of Anekant. With this book, he will bring to our world new spiritual riches, which are the most important riches of all.

Paul de Leeuw is Director of the Japanese Dutch Shinzen Foundation in Amsterdam.

www.shinto.nl

Acknowledgements

Many people have contributed to the making of this book, through everything from long-term moral support to spontaneous comments that inspire creative thought. In particular, I wish to thank Lynne Sedgmore CBE for consistent encouragement and for living out so many of the principles I have tried to describe in these pages. The Centre for Excellence in Leadership, of which she was until recently Director, is an example of Many-Sidedness in action. I also owe a debt of gratitude to Anant Shah, of the Meghraj Foundation, for his friendship, support and quiet, gentle encouragement.

It was Dr Atul Keshavji Shah, Chief Executive Officer of Diverse Ethics, who first introduced me to the concept of Anekant. Atul's steadfast friendship and profound understanding of Jainism have inspired me for many years. Similar encouragement has come from Elizabeth Medler, secretary of The Hamblin Trust and editor of *New Vision* magazine, along with Colyn Boyce and Edi Bilimoria of the Theosophical Society, whose questions and comments have helped me organize my ideas. My publisher, John Hunt, has supported me in this project with an infectious enthusiasm even when I was at my most despondent. I am grateful to Richard Stephenson for providing me with a bolt hole in Paris when I was in the final phase of my writing.

Almost all this book was written during the presidency of George W. Bush. His statement 'either you're with us or against us' expressed with surprising clarity everything that is wrong with our current political system. As such, it inspired me to write this book and it would be churlish not to admit my gratitude.

Author Note

The terms 'Anekant' and 'Many-Sidedness' are used interchangeably throughout the book.

Chapter 1

Introduction: Letting Go of Dogma

The final draft of this book was submitted for publication days before the inauguration of President Barack Obama in the United States. His election is in itself the most momentous event for Americans of this generation. It is therefore tempting for all of us, whatever our nationality and wherever we are in the world, to project all our hopes and dreams onto the new President. That is a burden impossible for even the most enlightened human being to bear, and at the time of writing we can only guess at what the Obama presidency will be like. However there was one brief snatch of radio commentary that stuck in my mind because it relates so directly and profoundly to the theme of this book.

In the radio discussion, a former colleague at the University of Chicago spoke of Barack Obama's participation at a conference as a young academic. He described a man who remained quiet and thoughtful for the first two days, whilst others disputed. He then contributed extensively, but those contributions took the form not of argument but of finding common factors or connecting strands between opposing arguments. Put simply: 'John is advocating Argument X, Mary is opposing him with Argument Y, but they both agree on Proposition Z.' If this approach is translated into a leadership strategy, it will be a form of leadership that has become unfamiliar to the west and to the world in general.

Whatever the form of government, democratic or dictatorial, 'strong leadership' has come to be equated with the forcible imprinting on the population of a 'policy agenda' based on one-sided ideology, with little or no regard for opponents or critics: any such regard is equated with 'weakness' or 'giving in'.

1

Opposition leadership, in turn, is equated with 'rubbishing' or sometimes subverting the actions and plans of those in power, with a view to 'capturing' power and using it in similarly one-sided and self-serving ways. Paradoxically, the attachment to this form of adversarial politics has if anything increased as the world has become more obviously complex and less reducible to simplistic formulae or ideological slogans. And, as it becomes clearer that we live in a world of connected parts, politically, economically and (above all) ecologically, the tendency towards compartmentalization and retrenchment has intensified.

Both of these responses are essentially fear reactions. This suggests that the root of adversarial politics is fear, rather than strength. War and terrorism are both logical conclusions of the adversarial method. They are extreme expressions of a mentality that values division over integration. The adversarial approach is proving to be a remarkably inefficient and dangerous way of addressing problems, whether at national or global – or indeed local – levels. A truly radical, truly 'strong' form of politics is a politics of healing, in which Proposition Z transcends Arguments X and Y. It is well known that as a community organizer, Barack Obama was influenced strongly by the thought, as well as the practice, of Martin Luther King, Jr and the civil rights movement. King, in turn, was strongly influenced by Mahatma Gandhi, whose strategy of 'non-violent non-co-operation' with British colonialism he adapted to opposing racial segregation and social injustice. The example of Gandhi's *Satyagraha* ('truth struggle') proves that non-violence is *not* the same as compromise but has a spirit of resolution and ethical clarity that more conventional strategies lack.

A devout Hindu, Gandhi was nonetheless strongly impressed by the teachings of Jainism, a parallel and equally ancient stream of Indic thought from which the idea of Many-Sidedness comes to us. Jain teachings encouraged him to place non-violence (also part of the 'eternal tradition' of Hindu wisdom) at the centre of his political and social philosophy. That philosophy was also about living in greater harmony with the rhythms and cycles of nature rather than trying to dominate them, and being ourselves less dominated by machines and impersonal bureaucratic processes.

Many-Sidedness, the subject of this book, is the ability to move beyond X and Y to arrive at Z. In Jainism, it is far more than a political strategy, but part of a spiritual quest or truth struggle towards understanding of our true needs, as individuals and as a species, and our place in the universe. It is a spirituality based on compassion, restraint and learning to make full and creative use of human intelligence. For Jains, that is not the same as continuous territorial economic expansion or attempts at human dominance – whether of other humans, other species or the planet's resources. In fact it is the opposite: a process of learning to live within limits and cultivating the inner life, the life of the mind and spirit. Much of this book was researched during a period of so-called growth. The current economic downturn reminds us painfully of the transient, illusory nature of material attachments. Let us hope that the solutions we find involve new ways of living and thinking rather than attempts to revive lost illusions. Here, the principle and practice of Many-Sidedness can help us, for it involves a process of constant questioning of received assumptions, as well as our own thoughts, opinions and motives.

Jains understand that there is a connection between materialism – the idea that we must always have more 'things' – and the dogmatic clinging to ideological dogmas which we attempt to impose on others. Both involve illusions of power and both are the products of 'attachment'. We cling to accumulated objects and we cling to ideas in an attempt to achieve security and well-being, while really only harming ourselves and others. The key to spiritual advancement is the abandonment of attachment, the process of 'letting go'. By so doing, we gain a sense of

3

perspective and recognize that no single human idea, any more than any single human being, has 'all' the answers and that despite our intelligence we are only an infinitesimal force within the vastness of the universe.

True to the spirit of Many-Sidedness, this book both is and is not a book about Jainism, just as it is and is not a book about politics. It is about Jainism, in the sense that the idea at its core, that of Anekantavada (Anekant), or Many-Sidedness, lies at the heart of Jain doctrine. Yet the collection of ideas that we conveniently describe as 'Jain' are also primal human ideas and goals. They have been preserved for millennia by a unique and rich form of Indic wisdom, the Jain *dharma* or path, but they remain just below the level of consciousness across the spectrum of human cultures, and are at the root of all the great spiritual systems of humankind. These ideas can be summarized as non-violence and living within the limits and rhythms of nature. They resonate through the ages and could be said to have a special resonance today, as we search for ways to reconcile cultural differences (perceived and real) and address ecological problems that stem, at least in part, from human arrogance.

Anekant, the non-violence of the mind, is one of the oldest human ideas. At the same time, it takes us beyond our humanity and reconnects us with all living systems. It offers us a means to resolve the conflicts within ourselves, themselves reflections of the division between humanity and nature, which results from illusions of power and dominance. Many-Sidedness can help us heal the wounds that have arisen out of misguided notions of 'progress' and the idea that nature exists to be 'conquered' and exploited. Exploitation of nature, and other species, is linked closely to the exploitation of fellow humans. The justifications for all forms of exploitation are essentially the same. Many-Sidedness offers a way beyond the exploitative mentality. It is about the conquest of the self by letting go of attachments, be they to material possessions or to dogmatic patterns of thought.

It teaches us that intelligence is not the same as domination and that true power is not about separation and conflict, but co-operation with all beings.

Jain teachings are a repository of these ideas, which belong to us all. And so the ideas in the book are based on Jainism, but have equal relevance to non-Jains, including myself. In the same way, perhaps, the intention of the book is political but also free from politics. It has no party line, it has no blueprint and imposes no solutions. However, it offers a different way of looking at politics, which points us beyond adversarial divisions and asks us to let go of doctrinaire certainties and other forms of mental violence.

Anekant has been described as 'the third eye' by one of the leading modern teachers of Jainism, Acharya (spiritual leader) Mahapragya. This is because it enables us to see beneath the surface of consciousness, to find the hidden connections that are not obvious or immediately visible. It is also a synthesis of all subjective visions of the world, which become parts of something far larger than themselves. The third eye lights our path towards the truth, but offers no shortcuts. Enlightenment, or even awakening, can take many lifetimes, and so our attitude must always be one of humility and questioning – of ourselves and our motives, more than those of others.

The doctrine of Many-Sidedness is one of the greatest jewels of Indic civilization. It is fitting that as India emerges as a player on the global stage, the light should be shone on this spiritual treasure as well.

Chapter 2

A Subtle Power

Only connect!
E.M. Forster

Water from the ocean contained in a pot can neither be called
an ocean nor a non-ocean, but only a part of the ocean.
Similarly, a doctrine, though arising from absolute can
neither be called a whole truth nor a non-truth.
Acharya Vidyandi, eleventh-century CE Jain spiritual leader

Truth is Something Different

There was once a group of blind men who approached an elephant in the forest. One of them touched the animal's ears and perceived a flat, fan-like creature. Another man touched the leg and found a thick, round post and yet another found the trunk and thought the elephant was like a long, hairy rope. Finally the owner of the elephant said to them: 'All of you are correct, but you are also wrong because each of you has touched only one side of the elephant. Each of you is right from your individual standpoint, but the truth is something different altogether.'

This story is a Jain version of a well-known folk tale, of Indian origin, told in an infinite variety of ways by people of many different faiths. Sufi Muslims, for example, tell it to illustrate the subtlety and complexity of the inner life of Islam. Hindus tell it to show that the divine power can be viewed and experienced in any number of guises. In this sense, the story expresses in simple terms the essence of Indic spirituality: pluralist, tolerant and yet committed to the pursuit of truth. Yet this approach is also profoundly relevant to a world in which religious faith has re-emerged as a dominant force and spiritual paths jostle angrily with each other. The acceptance of parallel versions of the truth, or different ways towards the same truth, could be the only way to save the world from violence and tyranny.

For the Jains, a minority spiritual tradition in India, the story itself – and the fact that it is told in so many ways – illustrates a principle known as Anekant. This can be expressed in English as 'Many-Sidedness', or 'Multiple Viewpoints'. More literally, it means 'Non-One-Sidedness', or 'Non-Absolutism'. Anekant is the non-violence of the mind. Its reverse, *Ekant*, is the 'one-sided' thinking that is the source of fundamentalism and intolerance. There are various ways of rendering the word 'Anekant'. Its full expression in Sanskrit, the ancient language of India, is *an-eka-anta-vada*, meaning the doctrine or way of non-exclusivity. Anekant is therefore sometimes rendered as *Anekantavada* or *Anekantvada*, but its abbreviated form is common among Jains, and will be used throughout this text. It will be used inter-changeably with the English term 'Many-Sidedness', which is the clearest way of explaining the idea and trips more easily off the tongue than other options.

The idea that there are many paths to the truth is central to the Jain philosophy. It has been a survival mechanism for millennia which has enabled Jains to avoid absorption into the majority Hindu culture, whilst maintaining a positive relationship with Hindus and even accepting Hindu deities as representing positive principles of life. It also enabled them to live peacefully under Muslim rule, earning the respect of their rulers even though Jain and Islamic practices appear superfi-cially so different. Jains were a successful part of Indian society under the British Raj, where they were admired by Christian missionaries and colonial administrators. Yet Jain ideas played a pivotal role in the struggle for independence and Jains remain a successful and valued community in modern, secular India. In other parts of the world, including Britain, the United States, Canada and East Africa, a Diaspora have combined full integration with the retention of its underlying beliefs and cultural values. Anekant has been the guiding principle, a solution to living in a society – and now a world – of many faiths and cultures existing side by side, where compromise is necessary for survival.

Yet it would be quite wrong to view Anekant as merely a pragmatic device, an instrument of survival and a process of compromise. In the apparently comfortable west, it is in any case too easy to sneer at such things. Here, matters of faith and philosophy have become widely associated with 'personal choice', without the threat of forced conversion or the discrimination that has been the human norm throughout history. Anekant *is* a survival mechanism, therefore, and this has been important to Jains. But it is also much more than that. Far from being about compromise or the abandonment of principles, it involves stricter and more difficult adherence to truth than any absolutist or fundamentalist ideology. Anekant is more difficult because it involves the renunciation and dispersal of worldly power. It means learning to live with, and even celebrate, human limitations, as well as human strengths, and uncoupling the idea of strength from the idea of physical power or even intellectual forcefulness. In other words, Anekant is radical in the original sense of the word. The word 'radical' derives from the Latin word *radix*, or root. Through the mechanism of Anekant, the Jain philosophy examines human – and ecological – problems from the roots upwards.

Many-Sidedness also represents a new approach to thinking. That is especially true perhaps within a western culture that favors the labeling and classification of everything, and the idea of perpetual opposition: light versus darkness, male versus female, class struggle for Marxists, market versus state for econo-mists. The statement 'either you're with us or against us' attributed to President George W. Bush after the events of '9/11' has implications far beyond foreign policy or a specifically right-wing worldview. It is in fact a fair, albeit simplistic, summary of the western mindset in the phase at which it has presently become stuck. Our linear thinking assumes a straight line of inevitable 'progress', despite occasional aberrations such as totalitarianism and war. Progress is translated into ever-rising living standards and levels of consumption, continuous economic expansion and scientific advances that enable us as humans to 'conquer', 'master' or rise above the rest of nature. Our binary thinking encourages us to draw artificial boundaries between ideas. These resemble the arbitrarily drawn borders that define many post-colonial states and make them hard to govern because they lack cultural and historical roots.

Binary thinking also creates illusory divisions between reason and intuition, scientific method and spiritual understanding. This way of thinking is clearly reflected in the revival of fervent and pietistic forms of religious practice that scorn science, and the spate of equally dogmatic atheist books and tracts, equating faith and superstition, that claim to be grounded in 'scientific' enlightenment.

Such extreme manifestations of linear and binary thinking show that such mental processes are outmoded and have outlived their limited usefulness. There is a growing sense, usually expressed tentatively, that progress is a god that has failed, and that by denying the spiritual dimension in our lives we are suppressing something valuable, both in our world and within ourselves. The denial of the spiritual dimension is a form of collective neurosis, which seems to be connected to the breakdown of families and communities and the growth of casual and random violence, which the language of inevitable progress cannot adequately explain. More important than this is the alienation of humanity from the natural world, that arises from the denial of the spirit. Failure to recognize the sacred in nature, or to understand the connections between all forms of life, has led to the poisoning of the planet, with its life-threatening consequences for us as human beings.

In our violence against other species and ecosystems, we are doing violence against ourselves. Throughout the economically affluent but spiritually impoverished world, we are witnessing the rise of self-harming behavior, not only the direct infliction of wounds on the body, but addiction, eating disorders and substance abuse. Each individual caught up in this cycle of abuse has his or her own story. There are many social and cultural explanations as well, but it is also possible to see the self-harm as symbolic of spiritual hunger, the void within caused by materialism, and the wounds that, in the name of progress, we are inflicting on ourselves and our world.

The epidemic of self-harm could therefore be the most dramatic expression of our rising anxieties about the prevailing mode of thought, with its impact on politics, economics, science and the environment. After all, the system of values on which Anekant is based originates in the principle of *Ahimsa*: non-violence, or more literally the avoidance of harm. Ahimsa is the most powerful and enduring idea to emerge from the Indic tradition of thought. In today's world, it has radical implications for the way we organize our society and relate to the earth, and the priorities around which we organize our lives.

Fortunately, addictive and self-harming behaviors are not the only manifestation of our anxiety about progress. Increasingly, there is a rational and spiritual critique of linear and binary thinking, and their consequences for the world. Science and spirituality converge around some of the conclusions of modern physics, which point towards a multi-layered universe, its components connected by subtle patterns beneath the surface rather than straight lines or poles of opposition. The science of ecology points towards the connectedness of all life forms. Such insights are well-known to practitioners of the most ancient spiritual paths, and are reflected in the spiritual teachings of indigenous peoples. This is reflected in the popularity of shamanism, which offers the possibility of connecting with parallel levels of consciousness – the 'upper' and 'lower' worlds – as well as experiencing that closeness to nature that has been stripped from men and women in so-called 'developed' societies.

In politics, the green movement, in its many and varied forms, is challenging the idea that economic growth is an end in itself, to be pursued whatever the social, cultural or environmental cost. It is about re-embedding humanity within nature and learning to live with limits, for in doing so we realize our true strengths. Green politics is also about (or at least supposed to be about) the healing of wounds within human society caused by our disconnection from nature and consequent assault on all that sustains life. Ecological consciousness is much more than environmentalism: it stems from a realization that materialism means death within life, the suppression of the creative human spirit.

The critique of western linear thinking has led to a widespread turning to the east – an interest especially in Buddhist and Hindu teachings – as well as indigenous traditions and attempts at a reconstructed paganism. Ironically, this is happening at just the time when many eastern societies are turning resolutely to the west, importing ideas of rights that emphasize personal fulfillment over communal obligation and economic models based on relentless expansion. Within the Abrahamic religions – Judaism, Christianity and Islam – there is a renewed emphasis on the inner life and the esoteric traditions. This is in part a revolt against the formal rules and outward trappings of faith, in part a search for a richer spiritual discipline.

All these currents – green consciousness, the new spirituality, even cutting-edge science – feed into the movement broadly defined as the 'New Age'. There is no simple way of defining the New Age, because it is inherently inclusive, but its connecting theme is a search for ways of thinking and living that break with restrictive and negative patterns, be they psychological and emotional, or cultural and political. But successful and influential as the New Age has become, it is also frequently self-defeating. To many observers, it has become the butt of humor because of its over-earnestness and apparent double standards. Too often, New Age practitioners appear to have 'lifestyles', whilst others are getting on with their lives. New Age therapies, meditative techniques and interests become an extension of the consumer culture. Ancient wisdom traditions are reduced to the level of add-on accessories or 'choices' in the spiritual supermarket.

Green politics has suffered a different, but parallel fate. It has almost entirely abandoned its original aims of moving beyond the polarities of 'left' and 'right' and developing holistic approaches to economic and social questions. Instead, it has become part of an adversarial culture of perpetual protest and recrimination, a green strand in a 'progressive' coalition, less about persuasion and healing, more about coercion and punishment. And so attempts to break free from linear and binary thinking become caught up in the very processes from which they seek to break free.

Even, or perhaps especially, attempts at total transformation often achieve the opposite results. For example, some of those who have 'become' Buddhists or Hindus and adopt Indian or Tibetan names strenuously deny their western heritage and conditioning. In the ferocity of their denials, they are demonstrating the extent of their western-ness: they are locked into adversarial modes of thought in which one idea or system of values is placed in perpetual opposition to another. To many New Age adherents and sympathizers, this comparison might seem unwelcome, but clear parallels can be drawn with the

'Neoconservative' movement in American (and to a lesser extent British) politics. Neoconservatives are, in the main, highly cerebral men and women who have become disillusioned with left-wing politics. Yet, in the inflexibility and zeal they bring to conservative causes, in their pursuit of doctrinal purity and their belief in permanent, revolutionary change, they are displaying the same patterns of thinking and behavior that they followed as Marxists. Many supporters of the New Age and green movements have unwittingly done the same.

It is here that the Jain idea of Anekant, or Many-Sidedness, could prove most useful. As well as liberating western humanity from destructive, literally hateful thoughts, it can also provide the key to a new, eco-centric form of politics and spirituality. This can be achieved without anyone having to 'become' a Jain, or 'convert' to Jainism. Any insistence on 'conversion' would be paradoxical in any case, because the Jain tradition does not actively seek converts, since the process of conversion . Instead, it welcomes as an honorary Jain anyone who seeks to live as non-violently as possible and to live in a sustainable way, reducing consumption in the interests of the planet as a whole.

As noted above, Mahatma Gandhi was deeply influenced by Jainism although he remained a devout Hindu. The impact of Jain philosophy on his thinking shifted the emphasis of his Hinduism, so that he placed non-violence at the centre of his thinking and linked the goal of independence with social justice and the equal – and complementary– relationships between men and women. Also, Gandhi's non-violent *Satyagraha* 'truth struggle' in turn influenced Martin Luther King, Jr's civil rights movement among African-Americans and the valuable campaigns for peace and justice that have since stemmed from it. Therefore there is already a strand in western thinking and modern political thought more generally that is closely connected with Jainism and on which we can draw creatively. This has had nothing to do with proselytizing by Jains, but has evolved through subtle influence, the percolation of ideas rather than their imposition on others.

Anekant and Syadvada

In traditional Jain teachings, Anekant operates through a process known as *Syadvada*. Sometimes translated loosely (but effectively) as 'maybe-ism', Syadvada means awareness and acceptance of multiple viewpoints, and incorporating that awareness into daily life and thought. Syadvada is a mechanism of continuous qualification, whereby the thinker is able to maintain his or her position, but be aware of and reflect upon other viewpoints without dismissing or denouncing them. Traditional Jainism bases the process of Syadvada around seven viewpoints:

1. *Syad-asti*: Existence ('in some ways, it is')
2. *Syad-nasti*: Non-Existence ('in some ways, it is not')
3. *Syad-asti-nasti*: Existence and Non-Existence ('in some ways, it is, and it is not')
4. *Syad-asti-avaktavyan*: Indescribability ('in some ways, it is, and it is indescribable')
5. *Syad-nasti-avaktavyan*: Existence and Indescribability ('in some ways, it is not, and it is indescribable')
6. *Syad-asti-nasti-avaktavyan*: Non-Existence and Indescribability ('in some ways, it is, it is not, and it is indescribable')
7. *Syad-avaktavyan:* Existence, Non-Existence and Indescribability ('in some ways, it is indescribable').

Only the *kevalins*, beings who had achieved complete enlightenment and so moved beyond the normal human condition, were held to be capable of seeing all the sides to a question. All human viewpoints were therefore labeled *Syadvada*, or 'conditioned viewpoints' or *Nayavada*, 'partial viewpoints': there are in theory an infinite number of *Nayas*. Syadvada is thereby at once a description of a type of limited human viewpoint and a way of acknowledging its limitedness. Anekant is the way in which contrasting viewpoints or partial truths are combined into a whole. Yet because we are restricted by our human consciousness, which is not fully spiritually evolved, we shall never arrive at that whole, the underlying truth, but can only journey towards it. Therefore if we wish to approach the truth we must constantly qualify our own viewpoints and consider what is not there more than what is. We cannot know anything unless we are conscious of how much we do not know. We cannot believe anything unless we are aware of other beliefs and the aspects of truth they might contain.

The early Jains used the technique of Syadvada to negotiate between the competing (and usually larger) philosophical schools of ancient India. It is a method that can reconcile theistic and non-theistic positions: 'God exists and does not exist', depending on how we describe the divine principle. In the same way, it can reconcile the idea of the universe as all matter with the idea of the universe as all spirit: the two coexist and have equal importance. Change and continuity are no longer polar opposites, but principles of life that interact creatively with each other. Mahavira, the founder of Jainism in its present form, but not of the Jain tradition itself, told one of his disciples, Gautama, that 'the soul is permanent as well as impermanent'. The soul, for Jains, differs from the western conception of soul, in that it is a unit of life rather than something that exists 'after' or independently of life. In its embodied form, it is impermanent, because the body dies and the soul reincarnates. In its pure form, the soul is permanent, and there is a thread of continuity – the karmic thread – that it takes from one embodied form to another. Its individual experiences are the accumulated experiences of multiple incarnations, and the soul retains its individuality beyond its point of enlightenment, becoming a 'liberated soul' in its own right, rather than merging into a larger stream of consciousness.

This method worked well for the Jains, as a minority tradition, enabling them to adopt a conciliatory rather than merely disputatious role and win the respect of those on both 'sides' of philosophical arguments. It has also helped Jain communities into the present time to navigate the choppy waters of religious and sectarian disputes, and to retain a distinctive voice. Syadvada is at once the product of Anekant, a Many-Sided outlook, and the means by which that outlook is maintained and transmitted between generations. And as well as a pragmatic tool, Anekant is a coherent worldview in its own right, which recognizes that all viewpoints should be considered and examined and that dogmatic, exclusionary thinking is the principal obstacle to the search for truth. It is the principle of non-violence applied to the intellect.

Moreover Anekant, and the process of constant qualification that is Syadvada, are appropriate forms of reasoning for a world where disparate ideologies conflict and collide, where the more we understand, the more we realize that there are no clear and 'definitive' answers, only uncertainties, where science, economics and the visual arts all reflect the complexity of life rather than simple truths. And yet, simultaneously, we are aware of the natural forces that connect us and the common roots of human culture and spirituality. We are aware of our dependence both on our fellow humans and other forms of life, and that the certainties of the recent past, whether of 'left-wing' or 'right-wing' origin, are withering away. In questioning our values, we are practicing Syadvada; in looking for new directions, we are living out Anekant.

A Many-Sided approach frees us from many of the artificial 'choices' which our binary, either/or system imposes. For example, it is possible to be at once 'pro-choice' and 'pro-life' on the vexed question of abortion rights, when we shift the question away from abortion itself towards preventing unwanted pregnancies and addressing some of their causes, such as poverty and community breakdown. Over the past fifty years, we have been conditioned to believe that we must choose between community cohesion and individual liberty. The former represses the latter because it restricts personal choice, according to both the cultural 'left' and the economic 'right'. Yet we realize increasingly that individual and community are interdependent, that without a sense of community, the freedom of the individual becomes meaningless or destructive. Conversely, communities cannot hold together without a sense of freedom and tolerance. Either/or choice between individual and community leads to the dead ends of narrow-mindedness and atomization, in which individuals are isolated from each other. Many-Sidedness offers the possibility of both/and, in place of either/or. Unlike adversarial political debate, it points towards unity rather than division – unity, but not uniformity, because all shades of meaning and opinion are considered as contributions, and are not lost.

Many-Sidedness equips us better for a culturally diverse and multi-faith society than binary thinking, which assumes a monoculture. The artificial choice between 'assimilation' and maintaining one's own culture produces two destructive outcomes. Assimilationism often means the loss of distinctive identity, in which positive forms of social and communal solidarity are abandoned. Multi-culturalism, of the kind that emphasizes difference, has in practice led to economic or cultural ghettos, in which people lead parallel lives and have a hostile relationship with the wider community. A Many-Sided approach allows for both integration and the retention of culture. It allows for new cultural influences to enrich the larger society: the 'salad bowl' approach, as it came to be known in Canada, as opposed to the 'melting pot', which suppressed linguistic, cultural and sometimes religious differences.

At the same time, Many-Sidedness encourages the exchange of ideas between majority and minority communities, in which members of both can decide which beliefs and practices they retain and which they abandon. The fluidity of Anekant is well-suited to a world in which people and ideas move rather than remaining static. It is also better suited to a society in which men and women are full participants. The male and female principles are balanced, rather than being placed in a position of either/or conflict, with one suppressing or rebelling against the other. Anekant, in which there are many starting points and all experiences are equally valid, enables us to promote equality but at the same time retain and value difference, rather than letting one principle or one version of the truth cancel out others.

These are necessarily broad brushstrokes, showing us where a Many-Sided approach can begin and how it can be woven into our lives and help us live in a pluralist society. Most of all, they indicate an attitude of mind, which replaces dogmatic certainties with qualification and questioning, without abandoning the pursuit of truth.

Different from Relativism

Some critics – and proponents – of Anekant present it as a form of relativism, in which all ideas, thoughts and opinions are equal, and therefore there is no such thing as objective truth. This is a misrepresentation of Anekant, which is primarily about the pursuit of truth. Where the Many-Sided method differs from the dogmatic is in accepting the limitations of the human intellect. Therefore, if we are to get nearer the truth, we must examine all available possibilities. This approach is expressed well in a passage from the *Mahpurana* ('Great Legend') written by the teacher Jinasena in the ninth century CE, which concerns the existence (or non-existence) of a creator God:

> If God created the world, where was he before creation:
> If you say he is transcendent then, and needed no support,
> where is he now? ...

If God created the world by an act of his own will, without any raw material, Then it is just his will and nothing else ... If he is ever perfect and complete, how could the will to create have arisen in him?

If, on the other hand, he is not perfect, he could no more create the universe than a potter could.

If he is formless, actionless, and all-embracing, how could he have created the world? Such a soul, devoid of all modality, would have no desire to create anything ...

If you say that he created to no purpose, because it was his nature to do so, then God is pointless. If he created in some kind of sport, it was the sport of a foolish child, leading to trouble.

If he created because of the karma of embodied beings [acquired in a previous creation] He is not the Almighty Lord, but subordinate to something else ...

If out of love for living things and need of them he made the world, Why did he not make creation wholly blissful, free from misfortune?

If he were transcendent he would not create, for he would be free; Nor if involved in transmigration, for then he would not be almighty ...

Know that the world is uncreated, as time itself is, without beginning and end,

And is based on the principles [of] life ...

Uncreated and indestructible, it endures under the compulsion of its own nature...[1]

The text addresses from a Jain standpoint some of the arguments put forward by contemporary theistic movements within Hinduism. As such, it reflects a specific 'viewpoint' or version of the truth, as Jains admit theirs is. But the method is Many-Sided, because it explores and examines all possibilities as it works towards a non-theistic conclusion. And the conclusion itself is inconclusive, because it leaves us with so many unresolved questions about the nature of the universe. In other words Jainism, like the best of modern science, accepts that there is much that we still do not know.

It is worth noting here as well that, as a non-theistic doctrine, Jainism does not, in a simplistic sense, 'deny the existence of God', in postulating that the universe is eternal and – like energy – can neither be created nor destroyed. Jains often revere or indeed worship Hindu deities, attributing to them powers associated with emotions or forces within nature. On a larger scale, the divine principle is equated with the life force, which permeates the cosmos and is embodied in every life form within it.

More than that, Anekant is a tool of critical reasoning, as opposed to a bland acceptance of all ideas, or a 'post-modern' refutation of the very idea of truth. Indeed it is the opposite of the post-modernist approach, for its cautious search for truth is based on respect for the truth rather than debunking it. A Many-Sided approach is also wholly compatible with rejection of poisonous ideas such as racism. Rather than responding to such ideas with formulaic slogans or ritual denunciations, it seeks to address the motivations and grievances – and the ignorance – that lead some people to become racists. The aim is not to repress destructive ideas through physical force or rhetorical violence, because these quickly become just as destructive themselves. Instead, the ideas are refuted and examined, so that those held captive by them free themselves, or work through their negative impulses to arrive at something more worthwhile.

Even negative ideas are aspects of the truth, as experienced by some people. They can be condemned, subjected to criticism and we may (as the lesser of two evils) protect ourselves from them when they threaten us. But we cannot treat them as something external or 'other'. For in so doing, we conveniently avoid examining and striving to break our own negative patterns of thoughts, which, if we ignore them, become as dangerous as the ideas we despise.

Shedding Mental Karma

Anekant offers the possibility of a truly different way of thinking. It gives us the chance to break the repetitive karmic cycle that affects our minds and intellects at least as much as our physical bodies. The all too frequent descent of New Age practice into commercialism, and the descent of green politics into adversarial slogans, are both examples of karmic repetitiveness, as is the phenomenon of Neoconservatism. The accumulated 'baggage' of past thought, indeed past lives, pulls us downwards and traps us in the destructive cycle we are seeking to break. Anekant is about the shedding of mental karma, but in a spirit of calm acceptance rather than frenzied disavowal. For the Jain thought from which Anekant derives views existence as a balance between continuity and change, permanence and flux. The individual is a continuously evolving unit of consciousness, accumulating wisdom and experience as well as negative karma. There is a strand of continuity between each of that individual's incarnations. From the most apparently primitive organism to the most apparently advanced human, the same individual essence remains, as it journeys towards the enlightenment that is also a return to its point of origin. The spiritual evolution of the individual life force is not a straight line moving forward. Instead it spirals and zigzags, moving downwards as well as upwards.

In this sense, the individual's spiritual development reflects the universe of which that individual is a part, which passes through upward and downward cycles, lasting for many millions of years. Within this vastness, each life is simultaneously trivial and crucial: trivial because it is one among almost innumerable entities, crucial because it is intimately connected to every other life form, unique but part of something larger than itself and essential to the preservation of cosmic balance. The sense of perspective that such awareness provides can only translate into Many-Sided thinking. Anything else is unfinished or obsolete.

The new way of thinking represented by Anekant is cyclical rather than linear. It is about wholeness rather than compartmentalization. It looks beyond black and white towards the shades of grey, or rather the points where colors, like ideas, converge and overlap. It involves the equal and complementary use of reason and intuition, for it rejects the idea of a separation between them. In the same way, there is no difference between thought and action. Thoughts *are* actions and they profoundly affect the self and others. Anekant is a training of the mind, a form, it could be said, of mental meditation by which we acquire a greater clarity of perception and re-evaluate ourselves and our priorities.

The starting point for an understanding of Anekant is to think of truth as the summit of a mountain. Walkers can reach it by a variety of paths, some straight, some complex and meandering, but all pointing towards the same spot. Not everyone is strong enough to reach it, in fact comparatively few ever succeed, but all try to get as far as they can and might make many attempts, getting nearer the summit each time and trying different paths. Those who see reaching the summit as an act of 'conquest' are likely to be 'defeated' by the mountain and might fall from great heights. Some will reach the summit but see nothing because it is shrouded in mist. Those who are making the journey, by whatever route and whatever their level of skill or ambition, are obliged by the ethical code of hikers and mountaineers to respect and, where necessary, help others, and above all to respect the mountain as a living entity rather than an object to be controlled or dominated.

As they move upwards, the walkers become aware of a higher power, benign yet potentially overwhelming. This power transcends all their narrow concerns and interests, and everything that divides human beings from each other, or from other creatures. It is the opposite of coercive power, which is not a real power at all, but a transitory and destructive illusion.

Jains also explain the mental processes associated with Anekant in terms of a cut diamond, with many facets through which the same clear light is reflected. From whatever angle the stone is held up to the light, the light itself remains constant. Many-Sidedness is not the same as moral relativism, or the fashionable post-modernist claim that there is no such thing as truth – which is itself a doctrinaire assertion. Truth very much exists, and the search for it is the real purpose of human and all other life. Yet most of us are very far from the perception of truth, and will take many lifetimes even to come near to reaching it. The more doctrinaire, the more 'certain' we are about anything, the further from the truth we are likely to be. A doctrinaire certainty that is *partially* true is more dangerous than complete ignorance, for two reasons. First, it is likely to lead to coercion of others – human and non-human – in order to impose that certainty. Secondly, it has a destructive effect on the doctrinaires themselves, restricting their intellectual (and spiritual) vision, corrupting their understanding with hatred and contempt for those who disagree.

It is out of sheer *respect* for truth that it is approached tentatively, with recognition that we are all feeling our way towards it and need to keep questioning ourselves as much as others. The illusion that we know the truth endangers us because it makes us forget out limitations and think that we have absolute power over ourselves and others. Human intelligence therefore imperils us at least as much as it liberates us, because it leads so easily to the illusion that we have the key to all knowledge – and the illusion that we are 'superior' to fellow humans, or other creatures. Knowledge is unlocked when we approach it with humility and are constantly aware of other possibilities. The tolerant approach of Anekant is based on respect for the experiences and perceptions of those who are journeying towards the same point.

Anekant has universal significance for humanity. But to grasp it in any meaningful sense, it is necessary to realize that it has evolved from a specifically Jain way of looking at the world. In particular, the idea of Many-Sidedness arises from the Jain understanding of the individual, the position of humankind within the universe and the relationship between humanity and nature. These will all be explored in greater depth in the next chapter, but are worth summarizing here as points of reference.

Sympathy with All Creatures

According to Jain teachings, the individual is a unit of consciousness or life principle that passes through many incarnations on its journey to enlightenment. This is also a cyclical journey, because enlightenment is a return to the point of origin, a state of being unsullied by material attachments or delusory ambitions. Each individual 'life' is one of these incarnations, a stage on the journey. It is not, as in the western understanding, a discrete set of experiences. Although every life is unique, it also arises from a wide range of accumulated experiences. These cross all the boundaries that we as humans often arbitrarily set, such as divisions of gender, race or ethnicity, class or species.

Each individual life therefore incorporates many aspects of the truth in its karmic or evolutionary memory. Some of these seem to contradict each other, and often these conflicts continue over many lifetimes, below the level of consciousness. Greater enlightenment involves an awareness of such truths – male and female, animal or plant as well as human – as parts or our experience. Such understanding makes us able both to know and feel other points of view. It leads us to a position that the Jains call *Jiva Daya*: identification or sympathy with all creatures.

We have already noted that in Jain cosmology the universe passes through vast evolutionary cycles, downward and upward, continuously reinventing and replenishing itself. The downward and upward cycles are known as *avasarpini* and *utsarpini* respectively. They are likened to wheels, the spokes of which mark out each epoch. They last for millions of years and are mirrored in the karmic cycles in which all of us are enmeshed. From this perspective, each individual life is brief and transient. The sheer vastness of the cosmos puts into perspective our desires, our concerns, our obsessions and attachments. Like truth itself, it cannot be fully grasped by the human mind and so it reminds us of our weakness and insignificance.

At the same time, that limited understanding gives us a special significance as human beings. For although humans are not inherently superior to other forms of life, they possess characteristics that point us in a spiritual direction. Human curiosity and human intelligence can increase our self-knowledge and give us the choice to re-order our lives accordingly. Therefore, although there is no guarantee that all humans will achieve enlightenment, a human rebirth is necessary for spiritual development to take place. Humans possess the ability to choose *consciously* to live according to the principles of non-violence and sympathy with all creatures. That same potential for enlightenment can also work negatively. When that happens, it turns human beings into agents of the most extreme damage to cosmic harmony. Humans can rise to greater heights and fall to greater depths than any other species or category of being. And what applies to us as a species, applies to us as individuals. It follows that human intelligence confers responsibilities, not mere entitlements.

One of those responsibilities is to be aware that all life on earth and in the universe is interconnected. We need each other because in a literal sense we *are* each other. This fact overrides all our apparent differences and all ideas of domination, suppression, division that we might entertain. It reaches beneath all assumptions of superiority and the false belief that we are locked into a state of permanent competition for resources: human against human, humanity against 'the rest' of nature. The Jains call the hidden connections between all life forms *Parasparopagraho Jivanam*, which translates as 'all life is interconnected'. This involves seeing hidden connections within nature and understanding that to survive, and achieve spiritual maturity, we must co-operate with all beings rather than subdue them or destroy them indifferently in the name of 'progress'. We need to accept that other species, and ecosystems, have their own perceptions of the truth which have as much validity as our own and can sometimes illuminate us. Above all, we must constantly remind ourselves that as humans we are part of nature, not separate from, above or beyond it.

Becoming aware of the mutual dependence of all beings leads us to an ecological perspective, based on the principle of co-operation with all life. We learn to work with the grain of the natural world, rather than against it as our dominant economic and political structures have done. These structures are reflections of Ekant, or One-Sidedness. The ecological perspective is associated with Many-Sidedness, because it asks us to remember that we are but one aspect of nature, not the whole of it.

Cosmic Law

The concept of Many-Sidedness is also closely connected to the Jain idea of karma. Karma is already quite familiar in the west as the universal law of cause and effect. It is at the heart of Indic spiritual teachings, but is understood well beyond India through the spread of Buddhist and Hindu doctrines. In the west, it has entered popular culture and speech and become a staple of New Age thinking. Karma is often likened to a web. Its invisible threads enmesh us all and connect all parts of the universe together in a common cause. Similar ideas exist in other cultures, for example among some Native American and Australian Aboriginal peoples. Ancient Germanic peoples of northern

Europe had the concept of *wyrd* or 'fate' that was also likened to a web and associated with the interconnectedness of all life. Karma is the continuation of one of the most ancient human ideas, but it is also an idea whose time has come. Both the science of living systems and our understanding of human impact on the environment are making us see the web of life as more reality than metaphor.

Jains also regard karma as cosmic law. But they also interpret it as a quasi-physical process. The life force, or *jiva*, is weighed down by karmic 'particles' composed of subtle matter. These encase and trap us in banal, materialistic concerns. They also obstruct our clarity of vision, preventing us from understanding ourselves or grasping the truths of the universe. The process of thinking our way to enlightenment is linked to the 'shedding' of karma. This means adopting more ecological or sustainable ways of living. But it also means altering our patterns of thinking to let go of mental attachments – the dogmas, narrow certainties and prejudices which stop us from thinking clearly and lead to violence. Thoughts count as actions of the mind and so, like all other actions, have karmic influence. The shedding of karma involves clearing the mind of violent thoughts.

It is here that karma connects to the idea of Anekant. Clarity of thinking requires awareness of multiple viewpoints and an attitude of humility in the pursuit of knowledge and truth. Anekant is part of a much larger process of calming the mind, because greater enlightenment arises through calm reflection, rather than stress. A process of continuous rethinking leads us to a Many-Sided world and away from the one-sided ideologies that create conflict, whether external or internal. This is not, as it might seem to many people in the west, a simple process of rejecting outworn dogmas, overcoming prejudices and ceasing to be 'judgmental' towards others. None of these are, in themselves, enough and all of them can lead to one-sided worldviews or delusions of intellectual grandeur.

Nor does Anekant mean the adoption of a vague, generalized 'tolerance'. Tolerance is part of the Many-Sided worldview, but like every other human idea it cannot be seen in absolute terms. Far from embracing moral neutrality, Anekant requires a conscious move away from exploitative relationships, in economic and personal spheres. The Jain emphasis on equality, including equality between men and women, is based on a belief in the potential latent in every human being. Every human has the ability to contribute to a larger, Many-Sided truth. Likewise, acceptance of multiple viewpoints and non-absolutism alters our attitude towards nature. Other species and even plants have their own viewpoints that should be respected and from which we can learn. Anekant leads to a repositioning of our attitudes towards the way human society is organized and the way we share the planet with others. Far from representing withdrawal from the world, it has truly radical effects on the way we live in it.

From a western 'liberal' viewpoint, it would be easy to equate negative patterns of thinking with – for example – racism, sexism, homophobia and discrimination based on class or caste. These are all of course highly negative and in spiritual terms are forms of destructive karma. Yet the contrasting liberal principles are no guarantee of enlightenment. In some respects, they can be more dangerous than traditional prejudices, because they often involve an assumption of enlightenment. At best, this leads to complacency and lack of self-awareness, at worst to violent hatred and contempt for others. Those who define themselves as liberal or 'progressive' are at least as likely as reactionaries to be motivated by considerations of personal power and the desire for dominance. Sometimes, they have internalized the prejudices they claim to reject. Frequently they adopt the worst characteristics of their opponents, including one-sidedness, fanaticism and intolerance – with the added ingredients of hypocrisy and double standards. Thus enlightenment and Many-Sidedness need not have any connection with political or social liberalism. They are beyond 'left' and 'right', positions which embody one-sided thinking.

Many-Sidedness is less an ideology, more a form of mental practice. Among other things, it asks us to examine the intentions behind our opinions and beliefs as much as we think about their consciousness. A power-hungry liberal, for instance, might well be less enlightened and more destructive than a reactionary with a benign respect for tradition. Just as intention influences the results of an action, so it affects the quality of a thought. In the mental practice of Anekant, we apply the most rigorous judgments to ourselves and are slow to dismiss the opinions of others. The calming of the mind and the defeat of fanaticism are individual inner struggles at the same time as they are social and political campaigns. In exactly the same way, the evolving green consciousness unites political perspectives with personal choices. The late twentieth-century slogan 'the personal is political' acquires a new meaning, more holistic and less self-centered than it became for the generation of 1968.

In a world that is at once more closely connected and more sharply divided than ever before, complex problems defy one-sided solutions. The ideologies of the west appear dominant, but even in the (so-called) developed world itself their hold is tenuous, threatened by economic uncertainty and spiritual crisis. There is a loss of faith in the ideals of inevitable progress and abstract reason, not because they are wrong in themselves but because their focus has been too narrow. So-called progressive values have neglected the intuitive dimension of human thought and over-emphasized the mechanistic and statistical. They have allowed the left side of the brain, associated with logic, to rule the right side of the brain, associated with creative imagination. Both have suffered as a result. The alienation of western humanity from its intuitive aspect is reflected in alienation from nature and the treatment of non-humans as objects without 'rights'. The realities of urban pollution, climatic changes and the extinction of more and more species are forcing us to think about reintegrating with nature, to ensure our own survival. In the same way, the growth of anxiety disorders, depression and addiction in the most supposedly advanced societies leads us to question our definitions of advancement – definitions which, it turns out, are based on the denial of powerful aspects of ourselves.

Anekant has the potential to be a tool of reintegration. It enables a rational exploration of ideas to take place without sacrificing the principle of 'sympathy with all creatures'. It enables us to work for social justice, locally and globally, but place it in a broader, ecological context. Anekant is profoundly humanist, because it is founded on a belief in human intelligence and potential, but it is not based on human supremacy. Indeed it frees us from the restrictions of human supremacism. This allows us to throw off the constraints of mechanistic thinking, which compartmentalizes and separates rather than integrating and unifying. In a world of failed ideologies, Anekant offers the possibility of a new way of 'doing' politics and economics, a new approach to campaigning for change – and preserving what is valuable. Specifically, it can help the green movement to break free of the straitjacket imposed by 'grey' politics, which it has failed to do until now, because its supporters remain locked into outdated ideologies of 'progress' and one-sided ways of thinking and behaving. Anekant can help us to integrate the political and the spiritual dimensions, which we have been conditioned as a society to separate, despite the rise of faith as a new global force.

A Gift from the Jains

To practice Anekant, you do not have to be a Jain, to believe literally in karma or reincarnation, or even use the name 'Anekant'. However, it does mean acceptance of a different view of the human person from the compartmentalized western view, to which most New Age practitioners and 'green' campaigners still cling. By extension, it means looking differently at the place of humanity on earth, and within the universe. For western societies, a move beyond human supremacism is a shift of consciousness as radical as the shift during the European Renaissance from a *geocentric* to a *heliocentric* perspective. When we recognized that the earth revolves around the sun and not the reverse, it altered our view of the universe and opened the way for greater questioning of the role of the individual in society, along with the relationships between the citizen and the state, the human and the divine.

Through re-embedding humanity in nature (and giving up the illusion that 'man is the measure of all things'), we do not diminish ourselves but accept a more expansive view of the individual that goes beyond traditionally restrictive definitions of the self. We can also approach social problems more effectively when we place them within a broader, ecological context and accept a more inclusive view of 'society' that goes beyond the merely human. And we can be better campaigners for peace and justice when we accept that the campaign is as much within ourselves as in the outer world. Indeed the outward struggle, beloved of political activists of all stripes, descends quickly into self-righteousness and tyranny if it is not matched by inner struggle, the process of constant questioning of the self. Anekant is an *inner* revolution, a process of personal transformation that has an impact well beyond the self.

To heal our wounded planet, and the wounds within ourselves, we need to become more like the owner of the elephant in the folk tale. At present, our resemblance to the blind men is the main cause of conflict, war and the despoliation of the earth. Their blindness represents a failure to connect the many parts of the truth and an insistence on partial truths, which become more dangerous than lies. Anekant is about making connections – between mind and spirit, for example, or between humanity and nature, environmental and social justice. Ideas are like ecosystems, connected by intricate threads like living systems. One-sided thinking confuses power with coercion, whether physical force or 'the force of argument', its intellectual counterpart. Many-Sidedness unlocks genuine power, which is non-coercive and subtle, like that of the elephant's owner, who makes connections between parts and sees essential truths.

Many-Sidedness derives from the Jain tradition of India. It is a specific tradition, rooted in a specific culture. According to its own terms of reference, it is one facet of the diamond, one path to the summit of the mountain, one approach to the truth. Yet the idea of Anekant can be seen as Jainism's gift to people of all faiths, and none, or even as India's gift to the world, a welcome non-material gift at a time when it is emerging as a superpower. To understand Anekant better, and integrate it into our living and thinking, we need to know something about the spiritual philosophy from which it comes, and why it is so relevant to us now.

Chapter 3

A Counter-Cultural Faith

*All breathing, existing, living, sentient creatures should not be slain,
nor treated with violence, nor abused, nor tormented, nor driven
away. This is the pure, unchangeable, eternal law which the clever
ones, who understand the world, have proclaimed.*
Bhagvan Mahavira, twenty-fourth Tirthankara
(Path-Finder) of Jainism

The Relevance of Jainism

*I adore so greatly the principles of the Jain religion that I would like
to be reborn in a Jain community.*
George Bernard Shaw[2]

There are between five and ten million Jains in the world today.
Most are in India, but there is an extensive Diaspora, mainly in
East Africa, Britain and Western Europe, and North America. In
India, they are one of the most respected communities,
prominent in the caring professions such as medicine and
education as well as in government and commerce. This success
has been replicated everywhere Jains have settled. Family and
community are deeply important to them, but so are the wider
human family and the community of all beings. Success brings
with it obligations to others, human and non-human, and the
responsibility to lead modest, balanced lives, avoiding
exploitation and harm.

Jain numbers are hard to count, because Jains are famously
reticent about discussing their faith. This is because they prefer

to live it out as a positive example rather than asserting principles or appearing to judge others. And because they know that we are all on a journey to enlightenment, and as none of us are yet 'there', humility is called for. Proselytizing and seeking 'converts to the cause' contradicts the principle of Many-Sidedness.

When they talk about their faith, however, most Jains will emphasize its antiquity. Its roots, they believe, stretch into the deepest recesses of Indian antiquity. Theirs is a continuation in its pure form of the primal Indic religion, which is but one version of the primal human spiritual awakening. At the same time, Jains will make clear that the philosophy they live by is fully compatible with modern scientific concepts. It is not a 'religion' at all in the sense that we have come to understand the term, but a spiritual science and a practical path for living non-violently in a complex society. It is a dharma, which in the Indic tradition has the double meaning of spiritual path and natural law or under-lying truth of the universe. As with the best science, rationality is highly prized, but only when it is balanced by intuition. Reason and feeling are complementary, intertwined and answerable to each other. When only one of them is present, there can be no insight. The starting point is the individual's reason and feeling, as we are all spiritual equals and no one has a monopoly of truth. Kanti Mardia, a Jain physicist at Leeds University, has compared the spiritual seeker to the scientist conducting experiments in the laboratory. Each person is his or her own guru.[3]

While Jainism can appear strict, even harsh in its demands, it is also the gentlest of spiritual pathways, in which the only absolute is to refrain as far as possible from harming other forms of life, human or non-human. Jains do not seek converts, but have precepts that they believe all spiritually aware human beings should live by. Theirs is a radically democratic faith, in which individual conscience is paramount. Fully compatible with secular democracy and political or religious pluralism, it is also in one sense unashamedly elitist. Enlightenment is reserved for the few, and usually after many lifetimes.

All we can hope for, realistically, is to become as enlightened as our limited mental and spiritual capacities allow us. Yet that is quite a large 'all' and so does not induce a state of resignation or fatalism. A lot is expected of human beings, because of the intelligence and spiritual powers on which we too often pride ourselves. At the same time, that combination of intelligence and spiritual insight confers on us opportunities unique among the earth's life forms. But these are not the opportunities that humans usually think about: the opportunity to acquire wealth for its own sake, for example, or to exercise power over others (including other species) simply because we have the physical and mental capacities to do so. Such behavior, and the ambitions that give rise to it, are seen as weaknesses rather than strengths, as failure to take advantage of opportunities rather than the fulfillment of our potential.

Jainism can justly claim to be the first truly counter-cultural philosophy. This might sound surprising, given Jain success in conventional terms. Yet the teachings of the dharma are a profound critique of the conventional trappings of power and material progress. These are seen as delusions that obscure our understanding of our true selves, as fetters that bind us mentally, physically and spiritually. Before Gautama Buddha, and many centuries before Christ, Jain seers warned their fellow men and women that the usual human desires were delusions, that hierarchies of class and race were meaningless and destructive, that outward conformity to laws, religious or secular, was not enough. In place of conformity and hierarchy, Jainism gives free rein to the individual conscience, which is the seat of true power, but this freedom is not license to be selfish, for selfishness is the ultimate barrier to the achievement of freedom.

The inner life is more important than material possessions, more important than outward 'success', more important than acceptance or exercise of authority. This involves an understanding that all our experiences, all our conventional successes and failures, even our spiritual insights and our most valued experiences of friendship and love, are transient and worthwhile only if we use them to accumulate wisdom. And that wisdom can carry us forward to a more auspicious rebirth, with more opportunities to cultivate our minds and spirits. Any ambitions associated with spiritual practice are directed towards future lives and the moment of self-liberation, rather than status or 'achievement' within our present state, and this creates a sense of proportion, so that our actions and concerns do not loom too large.

The counter-cultural aspect of Jainism is its conscious turning away from the power structures and material ambitions that characterize most organized human societies. Throughout their history, Jains have always spoken the truth to worldly power, namely that it is a transient illusion. Unlike many 'organized' systems of faith and practice, they have consciously avoided becoming an established power to which others are forced to submit, believing that truth can only come from within, through a balance of knowing and feeling. However they have also advised rulers of all kinds, through words and through example, to use their positions wisely and for the good of all beings.

This strategy requires awareness of the transient nature of power, for understanding this prevents the delusions of grandeur on which oppressive and corrupt rule is founded. Because its foundation is non-violence, the Jain dharma challenges all relationships of domination, whether they are based on wealth, ideas of caste or class distinction, men ruling over women, notions of moral or racial superiority and colonialism. All these are illusions, spurious rationalizations for surrendering to our weakest and shallowest impulses, which in our delusions we confuse with strength.

More radically still, Jains see through the illusion underlying all artificial power relationships: human supremacy. Jains are acutely aware that human intelligence does not give us any 'right' to control and subjugate other species and exploit them for our own convenience −or because we wish to do so. Vivisection, for instance, is as unacceptable from a Jain stand-point as blood sport. Although there are certain important differ-ences between the two practices, one being concerned with curing (human) disease, the other with inflicting pain, there is a fundamental similarity. Both are assertions of human power and both erect a false barrier between humans and 'the rest' of nature, which is the greatest human delusion of all. Reverence for life, which is the most overt sign of Jain spiritual practice, extends beyond animal species to plants, rivers, the sea, mountain ranges – all forms of life, all ecosystems, and all condi-tions in which life can possibly exist.

The Jain path must therefore be trodden carefully, taking account of all life forms, human and non-human, avoiding hasty or capricious acts that will inevitably cause damage to others. It is important to remember that each living thing is an individual, like oneself, at once unique and part of an all-encompassing network or 'web' of life. Like the idea of reincarnation, as part of the spiritual journey, the sense of being part of something much larger than ourselves gives us a sense of perspective on our own powers and limits. It compels us, for ethical and practical reasons, to act with compassion and care. The ethical reasons are centered on the sanctity, and significance, of all life. If we have the capacity to grasp this, then we have the responsibility to behave with restraint, to protect life and the environment, which is recognized as the source of all life, including our own. At the heart of Jain doctrine is the concept of *Maitri*, or friendship with all beings and universal love. Maitri is literally the heart of Jainism, because it expresses the emotional, intuitive side of a highly rational system of thought. There is also a highly practical reason for compassionate behavior: when we do injury to life we are also harming ourselves.

The critique of human supremacy by the Jains is a logical extension of their critique of all power relationships among humans. Peter Singer, the philosopher of 'animal liberation' in the modern era, argued in the early 1970s that consciousness of 'speciesism' was an obvious progression from consciousness of racism and sexism. The Jain standpoint is similar but because its basis is spiritual before political, its first emphasis is on human responsibilities rather than animal rights. The intelligence that gives us spiritual awareness also gives us the ability to destroy on a large scale when it becomes dominated by delusion.

There is a connection between the ethos of friendship with all beings and the Jains' challenge to conventional human aspirations towards dominance and materialism. Real strength is equated with humility, with knowledge of our limits as well as our possibilities and a sense of ourselves as part of nature and dependent on it, rather than controlling or 'conquering' it. The conquest important to Jains is the conquest of the self, which means freeing ourselves from the attachments that limit our thinking and make us harm others – and ourselves. By learning to work with the grain of nature, instead of constantly chafing against it, we lose the restlessness and discontent that act as spiritual barriers and restrict us to material attachments. We thereby begin to acquire the sense of calm that enables us to develop the mind and spirit and to practice compassionate living.

From the counter-cultural critique of power and material aspiration, through the concept of Maitri and the web of life, Jainism derives its idea of Many-Sidedness or the mind freed from artificial boundaries. Jains are aware that violence, whether between humans, by humans to other species or by humans to the environment, arises out of violent thoughts. These violent thoughts – like all other forms of violence – are also violence against the self, giving rise to anger, self-hatred (which is part of hatred of others) and neurotic anxiety. Within the Jain dharma, there is a complex system of human psychology. Its basis, however, is simple. The violent impulses that arise out of our vulnerability and fear are the root of all our negative experiences, individually and collectively, and of our dysfunctional relationship with other beings. Violence is the primal delusion, behind even the idea of human dominance. A violent thought is more than a precursor to a violent act. It *is* a violent act.

This is why a critical step towards self-realization is the calming of our mind. That means freeing it from violent thoughts and impulses, along with the ambitions and delusions to which they give rise. Attachment arises from violence and becomes a form of violence, and so by freeing ourselves from violent thoughts we also free ourselves from attachment, both materialistic and ideological. Ideological attachments – the belief that our beliefs are inherently correct and should be imposed on others – are as much a cause of physical and mental violence as materialism. Indeed such delusions are the basis for much of the political and religious violence that is making our world more dangerous and confrontational.

Ideological attachment combines easily with the delusion that the earth's resources are at the eternal disposal of human groups, to be fought over, conquered and 'used' indefinitely. Thus it is not 'religion' that is the cause of war, as is so often stated, but attachment: to possessiveness, human-centered world-views and the conviction that our beliefs are exclusive 'truths' that justify acts of force.

Jainism is conscious that belief systems and ideologies, religious or secular, can be based only on limited human experience. Therefore they can never express more than a partial truth. Such understanding should lead us to engage in a continuous gentle questioning of our own beliefs, along with the motives behind them and the experiences from which they arise. Awareness of the limits of human thought, and above all human capacity to be 'right', should help us avoid fanaticism, rigidity, prejudice and the attempt to impose our ideas on others or act as moral censors. The spiritual goal of freeing our minds of violent thoughts is good for our mental and physical health, as individuals, and can have an equal impact on the peace of the world, including peace between humans and other species, or peace with the environment that nurtures us and lets us live.

The ancient wisdom of the Jains comes from the earliest beginnings of Indic civilization. As with indigenous spiritual paths both then and now, the sacred was sensed, felt and experienced in trees, rocks and mountains, in the sun and the rains, in the animals and plants on which humanity depended. This sense of sacred nature was preserved at the heart of Jainism and combines comfortably with reason, philosophy and science, both ancient and modern. The rational and the intuitive are not divided, as they have been in the west, but two parts of a whole. They are reconciled on the Jain path because they lead the spiritual seeker and the rational thinker (who are really one and the same) towards the same conclusions.

Jain teachings remind us, as science is now increasingly doing, that when we attempt to overthrow nature we create a dangerous imbalance. This threatens the stability of the earth and its ability to sustain life, including (or perhaps especially) our own. Equally, they remind us that when our beliefs become attachments, which we practice fanatically but without compassion, they lose their integrity as beliefs and become pretexts for oppression. Jain teachings also remind us that material ambitions and the desire for power can never be properly satisfied because they are fleeting, transient sensations without cosmic significance but with the ability to imprison our minds.

These insights are all profoundly relevant to an age when humans are grappling with climate change – and other types of ecological fallout from our delusional obsession with 'growth'. They are equally relevant to a world in which the movement of people and ideas is faster than ever previously envisaged by humanity and is too often expressed through anger and violence.

There is much evidence of spiritual reawakening in many areas of the world and among diverse cultures. This is especially evident, perhaps, in the so-called developed countries, where there is an increasing ambivalence towards that 'development' and its consequences. The awakening is not irrational, as some secular fundamentalists claim, but a reasoned response to an increasingly complex world where the one-dimensional certainties of progress and growth have proved profoundly and tragically inadequate. To be truly 'modern' requires openness to ancient wisdom, which is why the philosophy of the Jains now echoes down the millennia and resonates far beyond its Indic roots.

Jains and Hindus

Jains regard their faith as the most ancient Indic tradition. This does not mean that other faiths and traditions are viewed as less pure, or less authentic, merely that the Jain dharma predates divisions of caste, political hierarchy, military power and the predominance of masculine values. Implicit in this view is the suggestion that Jainism originated before the development of agriculture and the concept of private property, and certainly before the idea of the 'nation' or 'state' with their innate tendencies towards militarism, conquest and territorial expansion. But it was not called 'Jainism' then and only evolved as a distinctive tradition when it made itself distinct from aspects of the Vedic (or Hindu) dharma which we now called 'Hinduism'. Therefore the question that often arises in the west – is Jainism a separate faith, or is it part of the Hindu tradition? – has no satisfactory answer in conventional western terms. The answer to each part of that question is simultaneously yes and no.

This is perhaps the oldest example of Many-Sidedness as a Jain idea. Certainly it illustrates the first principle of Anekant, that of 'both/and' in place of 'either/or'. According to the prevalent form of reasoning in western culture, it is necessary to 'choose' or decide between competing principles: Hindu and Jain, in this instance, 'left' and 'right' in the political sphere, 'liberal' and 'conservative' on social issues. Jainism and many other Indic philosophies adopt a broader view, in which different strands of thought are not seen to be competing but peacefully coexist or actively co-operate with each other. Therefore, the imperative to 'choose' between ideas is not present and it is accepted that apparently conflicting principles can be reconciled because they are aspects of a larger truth.

Thus Jainism can be seen as part of the *sanatana dharma* or eternal truth that forms the basis of Hindu tradition, *and* it can be seen as a faith in its own right. It can be seen as at once a faith, in the sense of devotion and transcendence of the world, and a practical philosophy for living in the world. It is both a specific culture, into which one is born and nurtured, and a body of ideas which have universal significance, from which anyone can freely draw inspiration. Jains do not acknowledge the idea of a monolithic 'God', but recognize Hindu deities as positive cosmic forces.

The ancient character of the Jain path is reflected within its modern and highly developed concepts of non-violence, or *Ahimsa*, the starting point of Jainism and also the ultimate goal. The basis of Ahimsa in Jainism is that all forms of life are closely connected and mutually dependent, and that even the most minuscule or seemingly insignificant life (microbes, for instance) can have at least as much strength and importance as humans. The idea of life, and the cosmos, as a series of intricate, under-lying patterns is part of our most original awareness as humans, but this first insight is confirmed increasingly by modern scien-tific reason, in a cyclical process that is familiar across the spectrum of Indic thought – whether Jain or Hindu, Buddhist or Sikh.

The Path-Finders

Complex patterns in nature and different levels of reality require interpretation. For Jains, as for explorers whether scientific or geographical, the task is to find and follow a path that makes sense. Individuals are required to make sense of these patterns for themselves. However, they can be helped on their way by those who act as spiritual exemplars. In Jainism, these are known as *Tirthankaras*, a word that can be rendered in English as 'Path-Finders', but which literally means 'ford-makers'. They are those who help us cross over from chaotic and disordered to calm and enlightened thinking.

There are twenty-four Tirthankaras. The first of these, Rishabha (also known as Rikhava) is described in early scriptures as a *Jina*, or spiritual conqueror, who lived 'many thousands of years ago'. He is a semi-mythical figure, sometimes referred to as Rishabha of Kosala and acknowledged in many Hindu traditions as well. Often, he is viewed as a manifestation of the god Shiva, who is associated with the cycles of history and time. To the Jains, he is the founder of a faith tradition and at the same time an ancient lawgiver who laid down principles that transcend history or direct experience.

Unlike most semi-mythical founders, Rishabha does not have a warrior aspect. Instead, he is the personification of non-violence. The community over which he presides is settled and peaceful, based on the cultivation of grain, in which there are cities, currency and trade, a legal system, marriage and extended family structures. He was given the title *Adinatha*, or 'First Protector', and introduced the 'seventy-two sciences', starting with writing and arithmetic, but encompassing astrology, the visual and plastic arts, and practical trades such as weaving and metalwork. He is said to have taught women the art of love, along with dancing and singing. In other words, he acted as a civilizing force, making his community kinder and gentler, based on a coherent philosophy rather than pure intuition.

Thus the kingdom of Rishabha is neither other-worldly, nor does it have a tribal ethos in which virtue is defined by the ability to fight. Instead, he is the wise lawgiver who tamed and transformed a tribal society into one that was ordered and peaceful – an ideal as relevant to today's world, 'developed' or otherwise, as it was to the peoples of ancient India. Rishabha as ruler can be seen as the archetype of the successful lay Jain, one who places his wealth and talents at the disposal of the human community, one who protects life and avoids actions that harm others. Yet in the story of Rishabha there is also the attempt to move beyond what is immediately practical, because attachment to the worldly is the cause of psychic harm and harm to others.

Rishabha identified possessions, and temporal power, with karmic bondage, and so renounced his political authority to begin a life of wandering and austerity, the aim of which was to harm nothing, consume as little as possible and avoid possessive impulses of all kinds. It is for this renunciation, more than his role as a wise ruler, that he is recognized as the first Tirthankara who began to give shape to a distinctive Jain teaching.

Whether he existed in a literal form, whether he really was a manifestation of Shiva, the first Tirthankara personifies the Jain path. It is a path that values civilization in its true form, but seeks to move beyond the values of the civilized world when these become materialistic and delusional. Rishabha's settled, peaceful community corresponds in character to what we know of the Indus Valley civilization of what is today northern India and Pakistan, for little is known of this culture apart from its apparently remarkable peace and stability, and its cultivation of grain in around 7000 BCE. Evidence from archaeology reveals advanced and thriving urban societies, such as the cities of Harappa and Mohanjo-daro, and suggests that yogic practices existed: surviving sculptures and pottery depict figures in lotus positions. This suggests that Jains are correct to regard non-violence, meditation and the goal of release from attachments as the earliest Indian ideals, and to see a clear line that connects their world-view with some of the most ancient human communities.

Rishabha Adinatha established the pattern of life and behavior for the twenty-three Tirthankaras who followed. The details of their lives are recorded extensively in Jain texts. Most sprang from princely or at least influential households, exercised authority and responsibility and then sought enlightenment by casting aside material fetters. It is a pattern common to Indic cultural traditions: the householder who becomes an ascetic, renouncing the commitments, ambitions and desires which, whatever their value, have constrained his development as a spiritual being. The householder in question is nearly always male, but the majority of Jains believe that the nineteenth Tirthankara, Malli, was a woman, and some see her as an exemplar of female emancipation.

Parshva, the twenty-third Tirthankara, is said to have lived between 872 and 772 BCE. He is the Tirthankara most widely depicted in Jain painting and sculpture and there is some evidence for his historical existence. His role, in a sense, was to 'prepare the way' for the twenty-fourth Tirthankara, Mahavira. Parshva kept alive an ancient flame of ascetic practice, renunciation and non-violence at a time when ritual and formality seemed to be taking precedence over ethics and when a highly stratified caste society was becoming entrenched. These comparatively new values were challenged, implicitly and explicitly, by the twenty-third Tirthankara, who attained *Moksha*, or liberation from material bondage, as a result and remains an object of widespread reverence and guidance.

Bhagvan (Lord) Mahavira (599–527 BCE) was a contemporary of Gautama Buddha (563–483 BCE). His original name was Vardhamana Jnanaputra, but the title Mahavira, or 'Great Hero', was conferred on him because of his subtle powers as a spiritual leader. Like the Buddha, Mahavira was born into the Kshatriya, or warrior caste. The Kshatriya ranked below the Brahmin caste of priests and intellectuals, but they were far more than warriors, holding most of the political and administrative as well as military power. At the age of thirty, Mahavira gave up family, property and worldly responsibility to lead the life of a wandering ascetic. During his wanderings, he took five personal vows: never to stay at places where his presence would cause inconvenience to others; the precedence of the spiritual path over all material considerations; only to speak in answer to questions put to him by disciples or seekers; to accept only alms that he could hold in the palm of his hand; and not to render services to householders simply to fulfill his material needs.

Stripped of worldly commitments, living close to nature but interfering with it as little as possible, Mahavira reaffirmed the original principle of Indic spirituality. All life is held to be part of an integrated whole, and when we do injury to life other than our own, we inflict equal damage to ourselves. This idea is the basis of what we now call 'Jainism', and in today's world is surely the starting point for any coherent green philosophy.

According to the *Acaranga Sutra*, one of the most ancient and influential Jain texts, Mahavira's parents were followers of Parshva. His previous incarnation had been in the divine world, also known as the *Vimana* heaven, where he lived as a *deva*, one of the 'shining ones'. Such beings can interact with humanity and nature – indeed they can include nature spirits – but unlike the western conception of God or gods, they do not have absolute power over the universe. The circumstances of his birth, as related in another Jain text, the *Kalpa Sutra*, are of interest for what they tell us about the interaction between the Jain dharma and the larger Vedic culture, and its complex relationship with the emerging social structure.

Mahavira was originally the son of a Brahmin, Rishabhadatta ('Gift of Rishabha') and his wife Devananda ('Divine Bliss'). However Indra, the chief of the divine powers (known in some

46

Jain accounts as Sakra), intervened and arranged for the embryo to be removed from Devananda and placed inside the womb of Trishala, a Kshatriya woman married to Siddhartha. This miraculous event took place at a time when the stars were auspiciously conjoined, and Trishala saw fourteen auspicious signs in dreams, including a white elephant with four tusks and the goddess Sri who was noted for her beauty. Dream interpreters revealed to Siddhartha that the boy would either be a great monarch or a spiritual leader who would alter human consciousness.

This story reveals several aspects of Jainism that are linked to the concept of Many-Sidedness. First, although the Jain dharma is widely defined as 'non-Vedic', Vedic deities such as Indra play an important role in its storytelling. They are not worshipped as gods, yet they are accorded influence and respect and regarded as vital players in the cosmic drama. This suggests that the continuities between the Jain and Hindu traditions were, and remain, as important as the areas of separation. Secondly, in the legend of divinely inspired surrogacy, Indra (or Sakra) strikes a blow for the Kshatriya caste, and this move signifies a larger cultural anxiety about Brahmin rule.

Brahmanism was seen by its critics as not only elitist, which it was unashamedly, but as more concerned with political power and economic expansionism than with the inner life. War and conquest were increasingly exalted, and respect for life had been undermined by the introduction of animal sacrifice to some (but by no means all) Vedic rituals. This expansionist outlook is exemplified by references to darker-skinned Indic peoples as *dasyus*, a derogatory term implying the 'blackness' of conquered peoples and their implicit social and spiritual inferiority. Such words were certainly not used by everyone associated with Brahmin spirituality, and have no connection with the teachings of the *Rig Veda*, from which Brahmin practice evolved. The emergence of racial hierarchies was a symptom of a wider divergence between spiritual practice and political organization.

The growth of militarism and the entrenchment of caste and racial hierarchies in the age of Mahavira and Buddha meant that the principle of non-violence was eroded. The very existence of hierarchy and caste domination was a source of harm, not only because of the social injustice it created – which ultimately depended on force – but also because it created an atmosphere of illusion, whereby consciousness of status impeded the spiritual journey. This status consciousness, as in our own age, assumed the form of complacency and acquisitiveness among the elites or the upwardly mobile, and resentment among the socially excluded groups. It generated divisions widely recognized as spiritually as well as socially harmful. Increasingly, spiritual teachings were reserved for the few and this exclusivity was based on birth or social privilege rather than insight or intelligence. As it gained power, Brahmanism increasingly denied access to the Vedas to women and to members of lower castes.

The term *Veda* derives from the Sanskrit term for knowledge, signifying both what is known as fact and what is perceived as the true nature of reality. The Vedas, as a body of knowledge, were transmitted by oral tradition from earliest antiquity. By the time of Mahavira and the Buddha a powerful educational system had evolved whereby this knowledge was passed from father to son or from master, or guru, to disciple. Restricting access to the Vedas to high-born males was therefore denying the overwhelming majority of humanity the chance to gain access to their true selves.

In response to these developments, a renewal of interest in the *sramanic* traditions of India ran parallel to the rise of Brahmanism. 'Sramanic' means committed to ascetic disciplines. These might include monastic life, periods of fasting and sexual abstinence, or isolation from settled communities. Always, however, sramanic discipline involved seeking a way out of material enthrallment and placing worldly concerns in perspective. Unlike 'established' Vedic education, the sramanic

paths were open to all – to women as well as men, to the unedu-
cated and illiterate as much as the learned, the poor as well as the
privileged. Mastery of sramanic teachings requires aesthetic and
spiritual sensibility as much as, or more than, an ability to grasp
abstract concepts.

Jainism and Buddhism are both schools of sramanic insight
and practice. Often they are presented as rivals, with Buddhism
representing the Middle Way between full ascetic renunciation
and acceptance of material comforts, while Jainism is seen as
uncompromisingly ascetic and even austere. Mahavira persisted
with austerities (*tapas*) and ascetic practice throughout his
lifetime, whereas Gautama Buddha modified his stance, but this
does not mean either that Mahavira was more 'extreme' or that
Buddha compromised with the material world. They chose their
individual paths, which arose from the same spiritual – and
social – impulses. In the case of Mahavira, this meant a powerful
emphasis on the interconnectedness of life, and the need to live
as lightly as possible on earth.

The ascetic discipline of the Jain *muni* (monk or ascetic) can
indeed be harsh, and is uncompromising in abandoning
attachment, but the path recommended for lay men and women
is flexible and pragmatic, as well as disciplined. It also includes
the crucial principles of tolerance, flexibility and continuous self-
criticism to prevent arrogance and self-righteousness. As it
acquired its distinctive identity under Mahavira, and in the
centuries that followed, Jainism did not define itself in
opposition to Vedic civilization, or even Brahmanism. It
presented an alternative way of looking at the world and the
universe, another way towards a truth that is hard to grasp but
which can potentially be reached by all humans, indeed all
beings.

The twenty-four Tirthankaras have attained full enlightenment, which has freed them from all attachment and made
them at once all-knowing and immortal. They are human, by

origin, but at the point of Moksha, release or liberation, they cease to be human and move to another level of consciousness. They have achieved the status of kevalin, the enlightened being that does not need to consume anything or move, for even the smallest movements generate karma. The kevalin is one who has transcended the cycles of birth, death and rebirth.

As such, the Tirthankaras are revered by Jains, either as images or thought forms, because they are seen as examples of outstanding individuals. All of us (Jain and non-Jain) have the potential to emulate them, even if we have to work towards spiritual liberation through many rebirths. The Tirthankaras are not gods, and so are not worshipped, but looked to in calm meditation for guidance and inspiration. They represent the spiritual powers latent in every man and woman, and the possibility open to all to free ourselves from *avidya* or ignorance (literally, 'lack of awareness') and material need. Jain teachings temper humanism with humility. They emphasize that human potential exists, but stress equally that to fulfill it humans must be free of doctrinaire certainty, social arrogance, resentment and the desire to coerce.

The Tirthankaras have been able to explore all sides of all questions. They are spiritual victors because they have realized that truth is not one-dimensional, but Many-Sided, not restricted to an elite but accessible to all who have the largeness of spirit to find it.

The Conquest of Self

Mahavira, Rishabha and all the other Tirthankaras are known also as Jinas. The word *Jina* means 'conqueror', and Jainism is the faith of the conquerors, the philosophy of conquest. A Jina is a being who inspires others to live in a balanced and ethical way, and above all to respect life. But he or she – perhaps more accurately 'it', because Moksha includes freedom from gender – is also a spiritual conqueror. This means that the Jina has won a victory over the superficial self, the ego, in order to release the true self. Spiritual development is seen in terms of a journey, but it is also an inner discipline, or struggle with the self, in which enlightenment is equated with victory.

The language of spiritual victory might seem curiously militaristic for a faith dedicated to non-violence and the pursuit of peace at every level, from the individual psyche to the global community. There is a possibility that the origins of post-Mahavira Jainism in the Kshatriya or warrior caste has a bearing on this approach, with the idea of conquest turned away from political and economic expansion and redirected towards the inner self. Buddhism contains similar ideas of struggle and victory and Gautama Buddha was, like Vardhamana, a member of the warrior caste.

Whatever its origins, the Jain ideal of conquest is the logical product of a disciplined world-view, but one in which the discipline is not imposed artificially but must come from within. It arises from insight, and that insight is transformed into wisdom by practice, patience and careful nurturing. Many-Sidedness, which superficially might seem to represent the opposite approach, is in reality the ultimate discipline, because it demands that we abandon cherished certainties in the same way that we relinquish material attachments.

Conquest of the self does not imply the destruction of the self. On the contrary, it is the realization of the true, underlying self, which is identical with the soul. For the Jains, unlike other Indic traditions, the individual self, the individual soul, is supreme and so the aim of spiritual practice is not the obliteration of the self, but a return to full consciousness. Our attachments to worldly concerns diminish our true selves and point us further away from true understanding, which goes beyond human words, beyond argument and 'one-sided' positions. Our closely related belief that we are above and beyond 'the rest' of nature, and have the right to exercise control over it, diminishes us collectively.

From a Jain perspective, both our personal attachments to material possessions, and our collective attachment to human dominance, are evidence of our limitations rather than our power. To release our intelligence, spiritual and creative, we must abandon these attachments, which are based on illusions that range from the benign to the downright dangerous. Self-realization, therefore, is release from grasping desire, or rather the awareness that grasping desires are ultimately meaningless. They are meaningless whether they are purely material, or take the form of political ambitions, or the idea that we can 'own' or possess another human being rather than loving that person unconditionally. The conquest of the self is the abandonment of conditions and constraints. Achieved through discipline and renunciation, it is the ultimate release from artificially induced stress, which is why it is identified with liberation.

Spiritual victory – the conquest of self – does not come immediately or quickly. It is assumed that it will take place through many rebirths, over eons. All we can do, as human beings, is achieve as much as we can for ourselves, not in competition with others but through our own personal practice as our abilities and circumstances permit. Thus Jainism is simultaneously rigorous and flexible, at once elitist and open to all. It is rigorous in that the austerities involve far more than merely simple living. They include celibacy, mendicancy, subsistence diet and living outside social norms. The ascetic path is not for everyone, but those who follow it are respected, perhaps envied, even by the wealthiest and most outwardly 'successful' Jains. Yet those who cannot – or do not wish to – follow the ascetic path are also capable of profound spiritual growth. Creative acts, whether in the areas of public works, scientific discovery, education, or business within an ethical framework, can all generate positive energy. Even if they do not lead to Moksha, they point towards a more auspicious rebirth and have an intrinsic value in their own time.

The conquest of self is a Many-Sided process, involving self-criticism, the questioning of values and the reordering of priorities. The mental attitude required is one of calm rather than zeal, for the liberated self exists in a state of pure equanimity. Jain spiritual practice aims for dispassion rather than fervor. The goal is an objective view of the universe that, unlike conventional western ideas of objectivity, is neither cold nor abstract but spiritually alive and self-aware. Jain practice therefore points us away from narrow adherence to doctrine towards an acceptance of many paths to the truth: one path, indeed, for each unique life form.

The Jiva: A Unit of Life

In the Jain dharma, the true self is known as the *jiva*. The word is sometimes rendered in English as 'soul', but this does not express the full meaning. For the jiva is not a part of an individual that 'lives on' beyond death. Instead it is the original unit of life. It is pure energy, and at the same time pure consciousness. The jiva is without form, but is fully aware of itself. It is the real self, unaltered by karma and not restricted by the cycle of birth, death and rebirth. In the *Acaranga Sutra*, it is described as follows:

> [The true self] is not long nor small nor round nor triangular nor quadrangular nor circular; it is not black nor blue nor red nor green nor white; neither of good nor bad smell; not bitter nor pungent nor astringent nor sweet; neither rough nor soft; neither heavy nor light; neither cold nor hot; neither harsh nor smooth. It does not have a body, it is not born again, has no attachment and is without sexual gender. While having knowledge and sentience, there is nonetheless nothing with which it can be compared. Its being is without form, there is no condition of the unconditioned.

This state of being is the point of origin for all forms of life, before karma gives them the shapes and characters we understand. It is also the point to which we aim to return, the end of the spiritual journey as well as its beginning. Thus the Jina and the jiva are essentially one and the same. This cyclical pattern recurs continuously in the Jain world-view. It seems to reflect the cycles of nature, of which Jains – and modern science – are profoundly aware.

The most important aspect of the jiva is that it is an individual unit of consciousness. In Jainism there is no concept of a world soul, or universal soul, into which all life merges. Each unit of consciousness, each self, not only survives and persists from one incarnation to another, but in a liberated state remains an individual entity because enlightenment is the achievement of true individuality, rather than its abolition or absorption as in many schools of Buddhism and Vedanta. However, all forms of life in the cosmos contain jiva, which is why each life form is unique but also closely connected to all others. When we show respect for all life, we are recognizing that in all life the same qualities of pure consciousness are embedded, therefore all lives are ultimately equal and journeying to the same source.

Karma and Reincarnation

The idea of rebirth, and a cosmic law governing it, pervades Indic consciousness. It forms an important part of Jain teaching, providing further connections between all living things and a path out of materialistic consumption, which is the principal generator of karma. In the Jain tradition, as in other Indic philosophies, karma is the cosmic law of action, cause and effect. It determines the consequences of all acts, good and bad, and creates continuity between one life and another. All life is enmeshed in a karmic web, but the doctrine of karma is far from deterministic, for it gives the spiritually conscious person the chance to take control over his or her own life. The goal is escape from the karmic cycle, and the way to achieve this is to reduce all forms of negative impact on others and on the environment. Reasoned and ethical behavior stem from awareness of the karmic principle.

There is also a unique view of karma within the Jain tradition. As well as a principle of the universe, it also exists in a quasi-physical form as particles of subtle matter which encase the jiva. Karma literally means 'action', and the jiva comes into contact with karma at the point where it begins to move. The Jina, or liberated self that has escaped from karma, no longer moves in any way: it is beyond action. Karmic influence determines every aspect of the way in which the jiva incarnates, including its shape, size, species and level of spiritual evolution. Humans, whose intellects enable them to understand the karmic principle, have a greater possibility than others of escaping from it, or gaining a more auspicious rebirth. However, each of us also has a destructive potential, which if enacted causes us to regress to the lowest stages of evolution.

All 'embodied' life, that is all life that is under karmic influence, exists within the cycle of *samsara*: birth, death and rebirth. This pattern will continue until the attainment of Moksha. Often represented as a wheel, the samsaric cycle recognizes the principle of evolution but applies it to the spiritual as much as the physical and intellectual spheres. It includes all of life, from those life forms that are least spiritually conscious to those most capable of development and ultimate transcendence. Yet there is no familiar and reassuring concept (from a western standpoint) of inevitable progress with humanity at the pinnacle. Reincarnation often crosses the boundaries of species or categories of being, for the wheel of samsara encompasses deities and hell-beings as well as the more usual earthly forms.

Samsara reinforces the underlying principle that all life has the potential to develop spiritually and become enlightened. As well as the ecological connection between living things, there is a samsaric link through the possibility of transmigration between species. Even the smallest life forms, plant as well as animal, contain jiva. Jainism therefore takes account of the needs of life forms that cannot be seen by the naked eye, which is why some Jain monks wear strips of white cloth over their mouths as part of the principle of *Iryasamiti* or 'Careful Action'.

The concept of karma as matter, which encases the jiva and obscures its understanding of its true self, is a metaphorical representation of materialism and its consequences. For the crasser the materialism, the more false the values, the more a human being is gripped by inner discontent, anxiety and anger. Reduction of karmic influence is achieved by the reduction of material desires, and so the process of escape from karma is identical to the process of surrendering attachments, including attachment to one-sided and divisive belief systems.

A Cyclical Cosmos

The samsaric cycle is matched in Jain cosmology by a view of the universe as a series of eternally recurring cycles. As we briefly mentioned in Chapter 1, these are likened to the upward and downward movement of a wheel, and called *avasarpini* and *utsarpini* respectively. These forward and backward cycles last for millions of years and each produces, at irregular intervals, twenty-four Tirthankaras. Each age can be said to contain within it the seeds of its own destruction and regeneration. It is divided into epochs, which are like the spokes of a wheel, and so there is a constant sense of regeneration and continuity.

That the Jains were able in the age of Mahavira to conceive of large numbers is affirmed by the most poetic renderings of the Rishabha myth, in which he lived two million years as a prince and six million years as a king, all of which happened millions of years in the past. Jainism's ability to conceive of vast numbers, and also of the infinite and the eternal, placed it in the philosophical forefront in the age of Mahavira, Buddha and Vedic dharma. The idea of cycles corresponds with much of what we observe and know about life in the universe, from the growth of plants to the development of galaxies.

The 'inhabited universe' is known as the *lokakasa* and was known by early Jain seers to be teeming with life – the embodied jivas, all of them connected by an invisible karmic thread. The lokakasa represents a level of consciousness as well as a physical reality. Liberated souls – or those not yet embodied – exist in the space outside it. This is a higher level of consciousness, where the truth in all its complexities is understood. The lokakasa itself has upper and lower levels, the homes of deities and hell-beings respectively. Humans inhabit the middle level, which is the crucial area of the cosmic drama.

A 'Religion' Without 'God'

Jainism is a non-theistic religion. Whilst it acknowledges the existence of deities and hell-beings, these are not 'gods' but agents of positive and negative energy that exist within the samsaric cycle. In other words, they are incarnated jivas just like anyone else! Moreover, humans can incarnate as divine or hellish beings and for different reasons both states are likely to obstruct spiritual development. In general, a human incarnation is required to reduce or break free from the impact of karma, because of the nature of human intellect and consequent spiritual potential.

The universe came into being or evolved spontaneously and without a first cause. To look for a 'reason' for its existence, and for the existence of jiva, would seem presumptuous as well as unnecessary to a Jain. Deities of the Hindu pantheon exist in Jain folk tradition as *devas*, or heavenly beings, but they are not worshipped and there is no supreme creator God (or Goddess) as First Cause. There is, however, a divine power, and that is the life force that is within all of us and connects everything on earth and the universe together.

Belief in that power gives Jainism its religious dimension. That same dimension makes it a rational and scientific philosophy of life. It is also in one sense profoundly humanist, if we break the false link in the western mind between humanism and human supremacy. Jains, lay and ascetic, do not worship deities with power over them, but instead contemplate images of the Tirthankaras. These can be mental images, or they can take the form of statues and icons, as meditative tools. Thus the Tirthankaras do not offer direction, but act as points of guidance, through which people realize their best qualities. They seek to realize their full potential as human beings, and in so doing learn to accept their limitations as human beings.

The Four-Fold Order

Within the Jain dharma, there are two 'four-fold orders', one cosmic, the other governing the arrangement of human society. They are represented by each arm of the *svastika*, an ancient Jain symbol depicting the universe turning continuously through cycles of time, the samsaric wheel and the original source of life energy. The human four-fold order was put in place by Mahavira as the spiritual community or *sangha*: male ascetics, female ascetics, lay men and lay women. The cosmic four-fold order is composed of the four *gati*, the destinies or categories of rebirth: *manushya* (human), *tiryancha* (animal or plant), *deva* (celestial being) and *nirjara* (infernal being).

In human terms, the four-fold order signifies the distinction between ascetics and lay people, who live by different versions of the same rule. Both are regarded as essential, in their own way, to the survival of the Jain dharma and so they complement each other, even if their lives at times might appear to contrast. The four-fold order is based on continuity and interaction rather than hierarchy and exclusion. In addition to this, it indicates the equality of men and women, and the complementary relationship between masculine and feminine principles. Both have the possibility of following the spiritual path to its logical conclusion. They should also be able to live in a state of balance and harmony with each other for the survival of the human sangha.

Likewise, the four-fold arrangement of the gati represents the balance of nature, the way in which different levels of experience complement each other and interact. The idea of an order of complementary parts, reflecting different aspects of consciousness or different spiritual practices, is a foundation of Many-Sided thinking. So also is the view of time and history as cycles, instead of a narrow linear progression.

As a representation of life, the four destinies and the Fourfold Order, the svastika is a central component of the *Pratika*, a universal symbol of the Jain dharma. The outline of the Pratika represents the boundaries of the inhabited universe, the hand an expression of Ahimsa, the ideal of non-violence and perfect peace. Above the svastika, the three circles represent the *Triratna*: the Three Jewels of Right Faith, Right Understanding and Right Action. The crescent demarcates the place of liberated souls, whilst the uppermost circle signifies the Jina, a fully enlightened being who has escaped samsara.

In the west, especially, the image of the svastika has become associated with a genocidal political ideology and movement of the mid-twentieth century. In both theory and practice, this movement represents the opposite of the true meaning of the svastika, which is an ancient expression of life, peace and harmony with nature.

Pratika

The Five Vows

The simple, independent, non-violent way of life propagated by Mahavira and his predecessors remains the ideal for Jain ascetics. Lay men and women also subscribe to the values associated with this ideal and attempt to live in as non-violent a way as possible. The quest for non-violence includes the calming of the mind to free it from passion and anger, as well as compassion and fairness in all dealings with others. Mahavira codified Jain values for his followers, ascetic and lay, into the Five Vows, or *Vratas*, which remain central to Jain life and practice. These consist of:

> *Ahimsa*: non-violence, non-injury
> *Asteya*: non-theft
> *Satya*: truthfulness, integrity
> *Brahmacharya*: chastity, non-promiscuity
> *Aparigraha*: non-possessiveness

Jain ascetics live out these vows in as literal a way as possible, withdrawing from worldly concerns and seeming (to outsiders) to go to extreme lengths to avoid injury to life. This position is not to be confused with Ekant (extremism or one-sidedness). It is a sign of humility, because the ascetic is conscious of his imperfections, his human flaws, and so realizes that he can always do more. Or, more accurately, he realizes that he can do less, for one of the purposes of the Five Vows is to reduce human impact as far as is practically possible. Lay men and women conform to a modified form of the Vratas, which is at once ethical and pragmatic. They have the responsibility of interpreting the vows according to their circumstances and conditions, relying on intellect and conscience because they have no priesthood to compel obedience or impose an official line. There are certain customs, most notably a vegetarian diet, that are virtual 'givens' of Jain culture, and are associated in an obvious way with the minimizing of harm. However, there is wide variety within Jain life, with an emphasis on restrained tolerance rather than censure, self-criticism rather than criticism of others.

The vow of Ahimsa, or non-injury, applies as much to the

treatment of animals, and even plants, as to fellow humans. It also governs our attitude towards the environment, both in terms of our immediate surroundings and the planet as a whole. The vow of Ahimsa is a vow to conserve and sustain life, in all its variety, because we – and future generations – depend on it for physical and spiritual survival.

Similarly, the vow of Asteya goes further than abstinence from simple acts of theft. It means avoiding exploitative relationships, economic or social, personal or political. These invariably generate negative karma and inevitably corrupt and injure the exploiters and the exploited alike. They also have wider ramifications because they are likely to occur against a background of social justice, environmental destruction and violence, as well as generating passions and anger that make spiritual development impossible.

Likewise, as well as the obligation to tell the truth – to oneself as much as others – the vow of Satya requires integrity and fairness in all dealings, including business and commerce. Bramacharya means celibacy for ascetics, but for lay men and women it implies commitment, respect and affection within intimate relationships, and the avoidance of promiscuity, which is inherently exploitative and reduces human beings to the level of impersonal objects. Aparigraha, or non-possessiveness, involves the practice of voluntary simplicity, learning to recognize what we do not need and can well live without. But it also has a larger social and ecological meaning, requiring lay men and women to reject materialistic values and minimize the exploitation of the earth for consumption or profit.

In other words, the Five Vows are all closely intertwined around the objective of non-violent living. Because not everyone can be an ascetic, the contribution of every lay person is equally important to keeping the dharma alive and allowing its influence to percolate. On reaching adulthood, lay Jains take the *Anuvratas*, or Lesser Vows. Those who become ascetics take the *Mahavratas*, or Greater Vows. In each case the five Vratas are the same, but they are lived out differently. Indeed in the lay world, each person lives them out in his or her own way. This does much to explain the high percentage of Jains working in medicine and education, practicing ethical forms of business and placing their wealth at the disposal of the disadvantaged, human or animal.

As well as honoring their commitment to the Five Vows, Jains strive to live according to the Three Jewels. For in these principles of Right Faith, Right Understanding and Right Action are balanced theory and practice, intuitive sense and rational thought.

White Clad and Sky Clad

The most important division within Jainism today occurred during the century after Mahavira attained Moksha. It is a divide between the majority *Svetambara* ('white clad') and the minority *Digambara* ('sky clad') orders. These names refer to the clothing, or lack thereof, of the ascetics. Svetambara or white clad ascetics (male and female) wear simple white robes, whereas the male ascetics of the Digambara order go naked. Their nudity represents a more literal interpretation of the vow of Aparigraha, in which non-possessiveness is expressed in its purest form. For reasons of practicality and traditional decency, women are deemed unable to behave in this way, and so cannot achieve the highest form of asceticism. This explains – and reflects – the differential roles accorded to men and women by the Digambara tradition.

To the Digambaras, women are neither inferior nor superior to men in the spiritual sphere, but they have physical barriers to the attainment of Moksha. Therefore, the most auspicious rebirths are inevitably male rather than female. Digambaras reject the idea that Malli, the nineteenth Tirthankara, was a woman. Their nineteenth Tirthankara, Mallinath, was male like all his colleagues. For the Digambaras, Mahavira was celibate throughout his adult life, whereas in the Svetambara tradition he was married with one daughter.

In contrast, the Svetambara majority admit women to all levels of ascetic life and do not regard nudity as essential to 'pure' renunciation. They regard discrimination on grounds of gender as a form of irrational attachment (as do the Digambaras in all areas other than this) and view every human being as having the potential for enlightenment. The Svetambara–Digambara divide should not be seen as a schism along the lines of Sunni and Shi'a Islam, or Catholic and Protestant Christianity. Rather than opposed factions, they represent two distinctive yet overlapping schools of Jain practice. Often, they share temples and other facilities, an example of Many-Sidedness in action. There has never been violent controversy between Jain factions. Individually and collectively, they have agreed to differ on the finer interpretative details and concentrate on practicing the Five Vows.

Living the Dharma

In Jainism, human beings are special only in that they possess a type of intelligence that can lead them to spiritual liberation. However, this intelligence can lead us to the nadir of destructiveness as well as the zenith of creativity: we can create concentration camps as well as great works of art; invent nuclear weapons as well as cures for disease. Human intelligence gives us responsibilities, to fellow humans and all beings, without which any idea of rights becomes meaningless.

The Jain way of life aims as far as possible to reflect these deep ecological concerns. Those who have taken ascetic vows are expected to abandon personal possessions entirely and live only on donations from lay Jains. They eat only to satisfy basic needs and practice Careful Action, or Iryasamiti. This means that they are required to examine every planned activity for evidence of harm to fellow creatures, and to avoid all actions deemed likely to cause preventable harm. The most powerful popular image of the Jain is the ascetic man or woman with a mouth covered by a length of cloth and carrying a small brush. The brush is for the ascetic to sweep the ground when walking, so that small life forms are left uninjured by human footsteps, whilst the covered mouth protects against the harmful effects of breath.

Such actions are the nearest any human being can come to 'pure' Ahimsa. In renouncing possessions and acquisitiveness, they are taking the vow of Aparigraha to its logical conclusion, which is also Ahimsa, because non-consumption is the same as non-injury to the earth. The purpose of ascetic practice is two-fold. First, it is an exercise in self-conquest as a path to enlightenment and release from karma. Secondly, it is an example of the conscious use of human intelligence to minimize harm to all life, played out dramatically to inspire lay men and women and remind them of their true priorities in life. Lay Jains regard the ascetic's life as the ideal of ethical and rational human existence. Even the most conventionally successful and wealthy among the laity admire ascetics above all other categories of human being. They hope that they will be able to take the Greater Vows at some stage in their lives or in a future incarnation. The fact that asceticism is seen as the highest stage of human development enables lay men and women to put all their mundane material concerns and narrow personal ambitions into perspective. And a sense of perspective is arguably the first step towards ecological living.

Few Jains are able to become dedicated ascetics, although some do so for limited periods in their lives. However, lay people practice Iryasamiti as far as practically possible. They are expected to be ecologically attuned, and to integrate that awareness into their daily lives and long-term plans. The Jain diet is vegetarian, to avoid the infliction of pain and death on sentient creatures for human pleasure. It is considered a duty to minimize waste, unnecessary travel, possessions and consumption.

Therefore, it is not unusual to find wealthy Jains who lead simple, unassuming lives. Charitable giving and philanthropy are powerful traditions, with endowments bestowed on schools, universities, hospitals and the famous *panjrapura* (animal sanctuaries). Ahmedabad, in Gujarat, is one of India's best-known centers for these sanctuaries. Even the sickest and most injured birds and beasts are nursed and cared for in the interests of Ahimsa and the sanctity of life.

Jains who have come to Britain and other western countries have retained their ecological consciousness. They are unlikely to proclaim their ideas loudly or immodestly and they most certainly do not seek 'converts' or the imposition of Jain values. Yet a concern with the natural world, with ecological and social justice, often plays a prominent part in their lives. In London, England, for example, a young couple called Nishma and Mahersh Shah has founded a catering service called Shambhu's, which provides and publicizes healthy and tasty international cooking that leaves a low ecological (and karmic) footprint.[4] Along with many other British Jains, Nishma and Mahersh support animal sanctuaries in the United Kingdom. These include Hugletts Wood Farm in East Sussex, on the south coast of England, founded on the principle of 'compassion for all life'.[5] Temples are encouraged to collect donations for Hugletts Wood, and similar causes, following the principle of Jiva Daya and the example of the panjrapuras. Also on the ecological front, writer and broadcaster Satish Kumar edits the Devon-based *Resurgence* magazine, which focuses on holistic and environmentally sensitive living.[6] Satish comes from a Jain family and took ascetic vows for several years as a young man.

Social entrepreneurship has always been an important part of Jain business life, in India and abroad. One example of this phenomenon is the late Meghji Pethraj Shah. In 1919, aged fifteen, he arrived in Kenya (then under British colonial rule) as part of a migration which continued until the middle of the twentieth century. Over the following thirty-five years, he created a financial services and real estate group, Meghraj, which is now based in London and operates in several countries in Europe and Asia.[7] From his retirement in 1954 until his death ten years later, Meghji Pethraj Shah devoted much of his time, money and energy to charitable activities, building schools, colleges and hospitals in India and Kenya.

In 2005, Dr Atul K. Shah[8], a prominent British Jain scholar and activist, has founded a company called Diverse Ethics, which advises businesses, public institutions and the not-for-profit sector on diversity issues. Atul's ethos goes beyond quotas and box ticking to an understanding that human and ecological diversity are interlinked.[9] Therefore, diversity programs make sense only as part of a broader culture of respect, which includes environmental awareness. This way of making connections is profoundly Jain in character, but can be successfully applied to a western, multicultural setting. The emphasis of Jain business activity is towards small and medium-sized enterprises, including co-operatives, in which commercial and profit-centered activity is balanced by social and community-based work. Larger enterprises continue to follow these principles, which have wider relevance. They offer a positive alternative to the one-sided capitalism that has contributed to economic crisis and widening inequality instead of the universal prosperity it has repeatedly promised.

Jain dharma extends the concept of 'society' to include fellow creatures, plants and the various ecosystems of the planet that support life. What better starting point is there for those of us – of all faiths or none – who seek a more balanced relationship between the rest of nature and humankind?

The Key Jain Texts
Among the best-known Jain writings are the *Acaranga Sutra*[10] and the *Tattvartha Sutra*.[11] These works are presented in the crisp style

of the Indian sutra tradition, as verses of philosophical import that act as points of reference for those who seek guidance on their journey towards truth. The *Acaranga* is one of eleven *angas* or 'limbs' of post-Mahavira Jainism. These 'limbs' together form a 'body' of Jain ideas. They were not composed directly by Mahavira himself, but in the several centuries that followed by *sthaviras* (elders), unknown men of learning who sought to ensure the permanence of Jain ideas in writing. The Angas carve out a distinctive Jain tradition within Indic culture, turning Jainism from an ancient wisdom transmitted orally into a faith that is recognized by others, with its own conventions and customs.

The Acaranga is the limb that refers to conduct (*acara*) and guides ascetics towards the best forms of outward behavior and, most important of all, the mentality that accords best with their vocation – based on humility and acceptance of multiple paths to the truth. It sets out explicitly the twin principles of non-violence and interconnectedness, which are the basis of Many-Sidedness or Anekant:

That which you consider worth destroying is (like) yourself.
That which you consider worth disciplining is (like) yourself.
That which you consider worth subjugating is (like) yourself.
That which you consider worth killing is (like) yourself.
The result of actions by you has to be borne by you, so do not
　　destroy anything.

The *Acaranga Sutra* is regarded as the oldest written portion of the Jain canon, dated to the fourth century BCE. It is written in Prakrit, a language written and spoken in large areas of India in Mahavira's time, a rival to Sanskrit with a more popular touch. Prakrit remains the language most widely associated with the Jain canon, but the *Tattvartha Sutra* ('That Which Is') is written in Sanskrit, the language most associated with scholarship and philosophy. Its use in this context is evidence of the spread of Jain influence beyond the sangha, and the desire by Jains to engage in dialogue with other schools of thought. Composed by Umasvati in the second century CE, the Tattvartha presents in three hundred and fifty verses the unique Jain approach to karma and liberation.

In Jainism, written texts do not represent articles of faith or even the heart of the dharma, but act as facilitators to good understanding and the right ethical choices. The idea of 'limbs' reflects the essence of Jain dharma – a series of intersecting parts forming a living whole, united by a shared life force. This sense of pluralistic unity gives a new relevance to the ancient faith of the Tirthankaras. By opening our minds to it, we are able to clear our minds of the dogmas that divide us by placing anger and greed above co-operation and friendship with all beings.

Within Indian culture, Jains have always enjoyed an influence that reaches well beyond their numbers. In the chaotically emerging global culture, they have the potential to inspire a revolution in consciousness, without firing a shot or even raising their voices.

Chapter 4

Karmic Ecology

Non-violence and kindness to living beings is kindness to oneself.
Mahavira

What is Karma?

Karma is a beautiful, compelling word that expresses an equally beautiful idea. Or, more accurately, it is a cover word for an intricate system of ideas and experiences. It is associated with the spiritual paths of Indic origin, but has found increasing resonance in the west over the past half century, as traditional certainties are dispelled, but new patterns seem to emerge. The term 'karma' has been simplified as it has entered the popular consciousness. In the west, it is perceived as a new and exotic concept, and it is therefore much prized on the shelves of the spiritual supermarket. A friend in Los Angeles, for example, described to me an occasion when a colleague spoke of 'bad karma' when her car refused to start. Admittedly, this is not a particularly 'green' example, but most of us can come up with similar instances of events that seem to reflect our inner mood or outlook, or which seem to be connected by a discernible (but not always rational) pattern.

Therefore it would be mistaken to sneer at people like my friend's colleague, for they display a greater intuitive under-standing of karma than most scholars of eastern religions. Karma *is* an intellectual concept that can be studied and analyzed. But it is also, at least as importantly, a lived experience to be under-stood through feeling rather than abstract reason. For the Jains, color, taste, smell and touch are all manifestations of karma, as is the entire range of emotional responses and desires. Holistic thinking does not recognize the division between intellect and intuition, reason and feeling. Karma transcends these boundaries. Therefore, it presents a radical and subtle challenge to the adversarial either/or patterns in which the modern, western consciousness has become trapped: humanity versus nature, man versus woman (or woman versus man), left versus right, progress versus tradition, civilized versus wild.

Karma does not 'do' versus. Within the human realm, it rises above and beyond all differences of race or color, gender or caste. More than that, it overrides the falsely comforting distinctions humans have made between themselves, other species and 'the rest' of nature. Karma reminds us that all beings, all ecosystems, are at once distinct and unique and part of a whole. Karma is the cosmic principle of connectedness. It is the process through which the continuity and interdependence of all life manifests itself.

The literal meaning of karma is 'action'. This makes sense, because activity defines life and every action by every life form has wider significance because it impinges on others. In the Hindu tradition, Karma Yoga is the path of good works that leads to spiritual understanding and with it a sense of unity with all beings, the cosmos and the higher or divine principle. The Jain and Buddhist paths are both viewed by Hindus as expressions of Karma Yoga, the Yoga of Action.

Karma can thereby involve a positive process of taking control over one's own life and living in a beneficial manner. It is more than an impersonal, cosmic law and it is not about fatalism or resignation, as it is sometimes portrayed. Yet from the Jain standpoint, the concept of action is far wider than we would usually assume, encompassing thoughts as well as the smallest deeds and vital functions such as drawing breath. All these activities are part of the bigger karmic picture, profoundly affecting our own lives and the lives of others, be they animal, plant or human form.

In the west, the artificial mind/body division has conditioned us to separate thought from action. Yet, from a Jain perspective, thoughts can often have greater karmic significance than overt deeds, sometimes even those that involve physical force. This might seem a strange and exaggerated view of the power of thought. But almost all of us will have come across those whom we describe as 'radiating calm' because of their positive thoughts and attitudes, and those who appear to be 'eaten up with hatred' or 'consumed with resentment'. Moreover, our own thoughts influence, and are influenced by, our physical and spiritual health. There are also many degrees of continuity between thought and action. Most obviously, perhaps, a prejudiced person is likely to express and act out that prejudice in ways that cause injury to others, whilst a resentful person is likely to be unkind. Positive feelings of friendship and love are likely to be expressed through benevolent actions towards friends and loved ones.

At a subtler level, the law of karma does not distinguish between intention and outcome. It follows that, in karmic terms, a superficially 'good' outcome might be just as destructive as a 'bad' one if the motive is malevolent or concerned with personal aggrandizement. Once again, this makes sense if we reflect that intention almost invariably influences outcome, and that seemingly good intentions are frequently corroded by the lust for power or ideological dogma. Thus, for instance, an educational system founded on notions of 'character building' that sound lofty, but in fact are twisted and perverse, is likely to produce maimed personalities rather than rounded characters.

Likewise, a top-down approach to social problems, without listening to or respecting the individuals and communities involved, will produce bureaucratic, impersonal pseudo-solutions that do more damage than the original problem. The example of high-rise social housing springs instantly to mind. When we speak of a 'do-gooder', we certainly do not mean one whose actions have positive outcomes for those around them. Instead, we refer to one who imposes his or her ideas on others out of personal vanity and delusions of grandeur, usually with disastrous results. Those who think evil thoughts can be seen to be poisoning themselves in addition to those around them. They can realize their full destructive powers, but never their full creative potential.

In all these instances, we are well aware of the link between thought and action, indeed that thought is a form of action that often assumes great power. This link is expressed politically through (for example) laws against racial discrimination. Along with fostering changes in behavior, such laws are intended to advance public opinion, or persuade people to question their prejudices and received ideas. Karma places thought under the umbrella of action, and it also shows us that small actions are as important as global events. The latter are, after all, most often the sum total of many local and individual acts instead of spontaneous occurrences.

Today, the 'Butterfly Effect' is well known among physicists and meteorologists. It is 'the notion that a butterfly stirring the air today in Beijing can transform storm systems next month in New York'.[12] That is the starting principle of 'chaos theory', which is not about chaos in the conventional sense of random disorder, but hidden patterns connecting apparently unrelated events – in other words, the karmic web of life. And so recognition of the Butterfly Effect is also recognition of the principle of karma, acting throughout the natural world, the 'inhabited universe', and bringing its disparate parts together. At the same time, it recognizes that, because all life is interconnected, all actions, even the smallest, have a cosmic significance along with far-reaching consequences. Therefore the smallest harmful act and conversely the smallest individual act of goodness are no longer trivial and particular, but universal, powerful forces. This is reflected in the Jain principle of Careful Action. This enjoins us to plan our lives so that we cause minimal harm to all beings. Careful Action is Ahimsa in everyday practice.

When viewed from the standpoint of Careful Action, such familiar concepts as 'think globally, act locally', 'the personal is political' and 'small is beautiful' show an understanding of the principle of karma and cease to be simply slogans. Karmic awareness, indeed, breathes new life into such concepts, so that they cease to be platitudes and gain a spiritual dimension. We recognize that our actions, choices and decisions, however apparently unimportant, have a universal significance. Therefore, we cannot surrender responsibility for our actions, or our failure to act, and pass it on to those we consider more powerful than ourselves. We cannot justify inaction and bad choices purely on the grounds that government, business or some other shadowy 'they' have failed to give a lead.

The starting point is oneself, for a change in the individual consciousness is as important, in karmic terms, as a shift of collective consciousness. Similarly, there is an intimate link between the awareness we show in our relationships with fellow beings – not just human beings – and our larger world-view. We cannot hide behind abstract theories merely because they appear to be 'good'. The idealistic campaigner who is callous, ungenerous or exploitative in relation to others lacks self-awareness and therefore generates negative karmic energy which corrupts or destroys the idealistic campaign.

Karma teaches us humility. It helps us to understand that although we have great creative and spiritual powers as humans, we are still one life form, one organism among many in a world and universe teeming with life. Karma therefore warns us against the arrogant, willful form of humanism, the error common to western humanity and the model of 'development' it imposes. This error is human supremacism: the idea that humans are a dominant force and so can dominate and oppress other species and ecosystems, which were 'put on earth' for our benefit. Human supremacism is both the origin and the ultimate expression of one-sidedness, because it distorts the relationship between humanity and nature. Such confusion leads, in turn, to distorted relationships between human beings based on separation and conflict, rather than co-operation and solidarity.

This distorted world-view is challenged by the idea of karma. The purpose of this challenge is not to return us to fatalism or passivity in the face of larger forces, but to offer us a truer vision of humanism, based on compassion for all beings, an awareness that human needs are far more than material in character. More than that, karmic awareness equips us with a sense of proportion, an acceptance that there are limits to human understanding and that human survival depends on harmonious co-operation with the earth and its species rather than the relentless consumption of resources and the assumption of superiority.

The idea of karma asks us to question basic assumptions about the way we behave towards fellow humans and this extends to the way we organize our economy and society. An understanding of karma points us away from the goal of limitless economic expansion, which is a product of human aggression and the attempt to control or dominate nature. We are inspired to question the cult of 'progress' as an end in itself, and the equation of progress with material attachment. In other words, karma undermines all established certainties and overrides ideological dogmas – religious or secular. It moves us away from the left/right, either/or choices of traditional politics towards a quest for balance and synthesis.

Whilst karma is about processes that encompass us as humans, it is not outside of human control. Rather than diminishing us, a principle that *includes* all of humanity, and all of life, enhances each individual human being, along with all the other beings with whom we share the earth and the universe. The interconnectedness and equality of all life is a process of leveling up rather than a program of leveling down. Unlike human supremacism, which propels us towards destruction of life, karmic awareness allows us to realize our potential for creativity and compassion. It gives us the power to alter our priorities and so transform our lives.

Karma is the universal law of cause and effect, reminding us that all actions have consequences, many of which are obscured from immediate view. It is at once the process by which all living systems interconnect and the overriding principle of connectedness. For the Jains, liberation arises when karmic destiny is first understood and then transcended. Their understanding of the universe gives us a theoretical explanation of karma and a method for taking control over our destinies. Far from being merely ancient and arcane, this resonates with our present ecological and social concerns and points us to a holistic way of living and thinking.

Why Karma Matters

Karma is the experience of being enmeshed in the web of life, the samsaric cycle of birth, death and rebirth. Samsara is the mechanism that entangles us in karmic concerns, but it is also the means by which we escape them. For each being, each unit of life is on its own spiritual journey through the samsaric cycle, spiraling towards enlightenment or veering away from it towards a lower form of consciousness. Every being, however 'elementary' it seems, is capable of spiritual development, an example of ancient insight mirroring modern understanding, since we know that seemingly primitive life forms are at least as complex as ourselves. Similarly, each human, however intelligent, is capable of regression and destruction. The more intellectually evolved a being is, the more vulnerable it is to spiritual catastrophe as well as creative insight and spiritual advance.

Moksha, or liberation, is identified ultimately with transcendence of the world, which means moving beyond an embodied, natural form and beyond the operation of karma. Yet within Jain consciousness, that re-embodiment is the point of transition between gross materialism, or lack of awareness, and the total understanding that frees us from karmic bondage – the 'mortal coil'. There is a vast spectrum of spiritual growth between un-awareness and enlightenment and it is within that spectrum that Jain dharma meets the ecological concerns of the modern world. We have seen already that the devout Jain believes in Maitri, or 'friendship with all beings'. The Jain ascetic on the threshold of enlightenment lives out that friendship in practice. Moksha usually takes many lifetimes to achieve and few beings are able to evolve to that level. Political ecology, at its best, acknowledges imperfection, even revels in it because it reflects the richness and intricacy of life. Friendship with all beings is its underlying purpose, for humans of all political or religious beliefs to find their own ways of working towards. This friendship arises out of the rebalancing of human beings with the natural world of which they are an integral part. Like Jains, ecologists seek to reduce the impact of human beings on their environment, not just for the sake of the planet but for our own inner well-being.

Karma is the means by which all of existence is connected. But it exists also in the Jain dharma, perhaps more importantly, as a form of subtle matter. Particles of this substance – which Kanti Mardia refers to as 'karmons' – adhere to the jiva and weighs it down in mundane existence.[13] Thus the life force, the unit of pure consciousness, is quite literally weighed down by karmic influences. For Jains, the process of accumulating karma is explicitly physical. Layers of karmic particles accumulate around the jiva, trapping it within the samsaric cycle so that it loses its lightness and thus its ability to move freely as a liberated and fully autonomous being.

These layers of karma are a form of pollution of the soul, pollution in the literal, ecological sense of the word. Karmic matter obscures the jiva's ability to perceive, restricting the clarity of its vision and, crucially, its awareness of itself. Thus karmic matter is an en-darkening influence, and yet, however heavy the layers that encase, the inner light of freedom is never fully snuffed out. The spark of enlightenment always remains alive and is programmed to find its way back, through the cycles of time, towards its pure, unpolluted essence.

Ultimately, everything is cyclical in the Jain dharma, as it is in the universe, and so the journey towards Moksha is both an evolution to a higher or superior consciousness and a return to the point of origin, the source of life. Layers of karmic matter correspond to false consciousness, the delusions and mistaken priorities that arise from material attachment, and lead to our committing injuries to life and living out of balance with the earth. The shedding of karmic matter is similar to what happens to us when we find new images within a painting, grasp a new idea, or gain an insight into a friend that leads to a better understanding of him or her.

Yet karmic reduction may be seen also, in simpler terms, as the equivalent of losing a bit of weight or clearing one's home of clutter, with the accompanying relief and sense of physical *lightness*. It follows that the conscious decision to reduce karmic influence corresponds also to the decision to abandon reckless patterns of consumption and live more harmoniously with others – to co-operate with all beings, including fellow humans. We can best understand the Jain concept of karma if we visualize a shadow or parallel self that responds constantly to our actions and thoughts, weighed down by some and lightened by others. We decide what we do to this shadow self, our subtle body, because it is a representation of our true self, and the patterns of karma we encounter and attract.

The loosening of our karmic bonds deepens our understanding of the true self, the light within us, and leads to a shift of priorities from material concerns to a sense that the ultimate purpose of life is spiritual. It marks a transition from indifference to those around us to the path of Careful Action, from aggression and passion to calm and inner contentment, from certainty to open-mindedness and respect for others. When we loosen our karmic fetters, we are also making peace with the world and our real selves. We move from a one-sided towards a Many-Sided view of life, in which our prejudices – in other words, our limited viewpoints – are challenged by reason and intuition alike.

Karma is a form of bondage, the entrapment of the soul in a materialistic universe of delusion. Yet the word 'bondage', and the accompanying process of karmic attachment, should not be seen in exclusively negative terms. It is more useful, and more enjoyable, to see the samsaric cycle as an adventure, a journey which includes much beauty and delight, much love and kindness, along the path to superior wisdom and self-knowledge. Karma itself can be positive and creative as well as negative and smothering. Although it always darkens the soul and holds it down, it can also at times point us towards greater under-standing or help us free ourselves from destructive patterns of life and thought. This is because karma is action, and so all actions, thoughts and desires are ultimately karmic, even the desire to escape karma itself and the practical actions we take to bring that about. In Jainism, the individual is engaged in a spiritual quest to overcome karmic bondage. This runs parallel to the quest for the ecological self which will lay the foundations for true social change.

The True Self as Ecological Self

Before we consider the way karmic bondage works, we should begin with the concept of self, which differs radically from conventional western notions of selfhood, with their illusions of narrow autonomy and their focus on competition and acquisi-tiveness. The point of origin is therefore the jiva. This is the basic unit of life, which is at once the primal form of existence and the highest form of consciousness. The 'inhabited universe' of Jainism is filled with jivas. Each one has its own distinctive identity. It is an individual in its own right, but it is without the characteristics we would conventionally associate with individuality, being beyond good and evil, without recognizable form or physical needs. And yet, as Tatia's commentary on the *Tattvartha Sutra* makes clear, all souls interact with each other, at a subtle level. Like earthly life forms, they are intimately connected, although they communicate with each other at a level of consciousness beyond word and action:

> Souls influence each other through service which may be favorable or unfavorable, beneficial or harmful. They cannot live independently of one another. They have to share their pleasure and pain with others. As partners in good and evil acts, they are jointly responsible although they must bear the karmic results individually for the part they play. They create a common environment and live together in weal and woe.

The soul exists as a unit of pure consciousness, and it is to this state that it strives to return. But it also contains energy, and this brings it into contact with karma and makes it interactive. This is where the jiva differs subtly from the Jina, which has moved beyond action and lives at a higher level of consciousness, the 'place of liberated souls'.

The jiva is, however, the true self. Its life is 'real' life, unlike the ultimately false concerns of material existence and the fabricated layers of personality that are the products of karmic influence. The jiva encompasses the western idea of soul, but it is also the life monad, the existence uncontaminated by karma and possessing clarity of vision. It is a unit of pure energy and so can neither be created nor destroyed. The individuality of the jiva, its pure selfhood, is defined by its all-knowing quality. Because it has not come into contact with karma, it comprehends everything and possesses full spiritual awareness. In Jainism, intellectual understanding and spiritual perception are one and the same, or two sides of the same coin. Part of the process of enlightenment is the reconciliation of mind and spirit. The jiva, therefore, is spiritually and intellectually aware, but it is detached from conventional moral considerations and choices, because even these are part of karma, part of the embodied state.

Power is karmic, too, therefore the jiva is powerless, unable to intervene in worldly affairs or directly determine its destiny. The life of the Jain ascetic aims to be as close to that of the jiva as a human life can be – without possessions, without political power, consuming as little as is practically possible, abstaining from sex and intoxication, avoiding anything that can lead to passion or anger. The lay Jain, who practices a modified version of the vows, attempts to avoid needless waste, act with integrity in business and personal relationships, show respect and give protection to all creatures.

Lay Jains might be outwardly wealthy and enjoy the trappings of professional success, but they are expected to live modestly and to use their wealth for socially useful purposes: the concept of social good inclusive of animals – and the environment – as much as fellow human beings. They are enjoined to use the talents of their present embodiments for the social good as well, which is why education and medicine are professions often favored by Jains. Such paths in life increase the possibility of auspicious rebirth, including rebirth as an ascetic. The ascetic abjures wealth and power, living close to nature and then retreating even from the natural world to live as minimally as possible. Meanwhile, the lay Jain sees wealth as only of lasting value if it provides the freedom to cultivate inner riches. But in the Jain world it is the ascetic who is most admired, the man who 'has' nothing but is far richer than his fellows because he is closest to his original self, his essence as jiva.

Self-realization is not about the assertion of self, as is too often the case in New Age routes to enlightenment. Neither is it, as in some eastern pathways, about the abolition or renunciation of individuality. Falling between these two poles, the emphasis is on distinguishing between priorities which are warped, misleading or corrupt and those which involve the cultivation of the mind and spirit, creativity and compassion – real human qualities – as opposed to the qualities promoted by competitive materialism and the pursuit of power, wealth or celebrity.

The 'conquering' ideal at the heart of Jainism is concerned with the overcoming of negative passions, including anger and greed, the conquest of ambitions to control and dominate others. It is, in effect, a form of spiritual therapy, through which the individual is asked to step back from his or her ordinary life and preoccupations, which tend in reality to be far narrower than those of the ascetic! Most of our priorities are concerned with ownership and control, not merely of possessions, but of people, ideas, and our own (apparent) status. This mentality translates, in politics, into ideologies of domination, territoriality and aggression – from racism through arrogant assumptions about the superiority of 'our way of life' to a righteous, pseudo-enlightened liberalism that dismisses the experiences of others. Philosophically, it results in the idea of human supremacy, the idea that the earth, and perhaps the rest of the universe, exists for our benefit, made up of 'resources' to be consumed, violated or experimented upon, rather than lives as valid as our own.

Becoming self-aware means renouncing, or rather becoming aware of the unimportance of, many of the things we are conditioned to associate with selfhood. It involves abandoning the idea of self as a rigidly delineated form in competition with all other 'selves' in favor of a more generous conception of the self, based on friendship with all beings, an ethos of co-operation and a sense of selfhood that takes delight in being part of something larger. Rather than being only a recognition of uniqueness and distinctive characteristics, an understanding of self includes an understanding of characteristics in common with all other forms of life and our dependence on all of them.

All life is bound together by its spiritual as well as material nature, in Jain terms by the existence of jiva. The life force gives us our unique characteristics, our innermost being, but also binds us together with all other life, so that, in Mahavira's words, 'we are' the creatures that we choose to hurt or protect, the humans we choose to uplift or exploit, the landscapes we choose to violate or conserve. Bill Devall, the American ecological thinker, presents a view of the *ecological self* that mirrors the spiritual ideals of personal restraint and respect for nature promoted by Jains. He refers to the North American legend of Sasquatch, or 'Bigfoot', the peaceful forest-dwelling primate:

> Some cultural anthropologists consider Sasquatch a legend which can be interpreted in terms of myth and folklore or in terms of the psychology of Native Americans. Other scientists say they won't believe in the existence of Sasquatch until they see bones or have a captured specimen.
>
> I see another possible explanation. Perhaps Sasquatch does exist – as an ideal. Perhaps Sasquatch represents a more mature kind of human, a future primal being. Understood in this way, Sasquatch has a fully realized ecological self. While we, who are children of technocratic civilization, must bring cumbersome technology into the forest to provide shelter and to satisfy our other needs and desires, Sasquatch dwells freely in the forest unencumbered by the burden of complex and complicated technology.
>
> While we are torn with desire for more power over other people and domination over nature, Sasquatch dwells peacefully and unobtrusively with other creatures in the forest. While we are dependent on huge bureaucracies such as schools, governments and military agencies, Sasquatch is independent and autonomous but also integrated with the forest.[14]

Sasquatch, by this reasoning, is simultaneously an advanced being who has overcome karma and a primal being, 'innocent' in the literal sense and living at peace with his surroundings. His way of life is quite similar to that of a Jain ascetic, or the forest monk of Theravada Buddhism, who lives as simply and as close to nature as possible. For the Native American peoples of the Pacific Northwest, Sasquatch was a reminder of the strength and power of the natural world and humanity's place in the web of life. For the modern 'civilization' of their successors, he is an archetype of spiritual loss, and at the same time a 'Green Man' figure who can restore our sense of connectedness. The Jain view of spiritual evolution as a return to the point of origin, the source of knowledge, is similar. It does not reject technological advancement or greater understanding of how the universe works. On the contrary, it respects them profoundly and so realizes that technology and the accumulation of facts are dangerous when they become ends in themselves and so fuel human arrogance. Then, they cease to be knowledge and become a form of ignorance, and 'civilization' becomes a façade concealing oppression and denial of life. The myth of Sasquatch, and the life of the ascetic, together remind us of a more expansive definition of self. As Devall argues:

> When sociologists discuss self they usually are referring to the social self. When asked 'who are you?', most people respond by saying: 'I am a Christian' or 'I am a male' or 'I am a carpenter' or 'a mother' or 'an American'. Sometimes people say 'I am an environmentalist.' A person expressing ecological self would say 'I am a forest being.'[15]

The forest is one of the most dramatic expressions of interdependence. When we are in it, we experience myriad diverse but intertwined life forms in their beauty and intricacy. When we cut it back, the ecological costs we reap are unpredictable and extreme, but we also inflict on ourselves deep psychological wounds, as if we are cutting off a part of ourselves. Yet within the forest, we can also become overwhelmed by a sense of isolation within nature that borders on fear, a feeling of uniqueness that makes us vulnerable. This is the spiritual dimension of the forest. When we experience it, we reconcile the self with the other, the individual universal, outer vulnerability with inner strength. The forest is a place where ecological and spiritual impulses overlap. As an ecological reality, it is crucial to human survival, and as a spiritual metaphor, it represents the journey towards the self and the conquest of transient concerns.

Self-realization is about identifying the self as part of an interconnected whole. It is also, inevitably, about Many-Sidedness. Nature and the cosmos are Many-Sided. Ecosystems have no doctrines, dogmas, or one-sided fixations. The spiritually conscious human, who recognizes the intricacies of nature and his place within it, is a practitioner of Anekant. The Norwegian philosopher Arne Naess identifies the exploration of our ecological self as an aspect of 'all around maturity', which Devall interprets as a 'many-sided maturity', although he makes no reference to the doctrine of Anekant.[16] When we access our ecological self, we acquire above all a sense of perspective on our place in the universe and the spiritual purpose behind our existence. We therefore cannot but be aware of the complexities of existence and the thread – in Jain terms, the karmic thread – that binds every smallest part of that existence together.

The journey to the ecological self is not really about 'empowerment', a word that is used so glibly that it loses its true meaning. Instead, it is about the dispersal of power, so that we work together rather than in isolation and use our creative energy to conserve and protect, rather than overpower and ravage. The Jain spiritual path is at the same time a withdrawal from and an engagement with the world. It is a withdrawal from what is *worldly* and superficial, but this stems from an involvement with and concern for the whole of life. In ancient times Jains recognized intuitively what ecologists recognize now from scientific proof. The culture of consumption, based on the narrow, disconnected 'self' and the violent withdrawal of humanity from nature, cannot sustain life.

Moreover, in the process of destroying life, we cannot attain happiness, contentment or well-being, whatever short-term material compensations we might gain. Those who think more profoundly about environmental concerns – Deep Ecologists, as they are sometimes called, or call themselves – look beyond immediate campaigning objectives towards a change of consciousness in which we re-evaluate our needs and wants. This includes re-examining the role of humanity within nature, and a search for spiritual (but not necessarily religious) values to counter-balance the materialism on which consumer society is based. In this, Deep Ecologists differ from single-issue environmentalists. In one sense, they form complementary parts of the environmental movement. However, the logical conclusion of Deep Ecology cannot be the mere patching up of existing ideologies and practices of human supremacism, but a Many-Sided evolution in thought that recognizes the diversity of life, rather than trying to impose uniform blueprints. As an intellectual and cultural movement, Deep Ecology is associated with thinkers like Arne Naess and Gary Snyder, the California-based poet and environmental campaigner. Although grounded in western preoccupations, it embraces other ways of thinking and being. Snyder is a Zen practitioner of long standing and Devall, who is also in the Deep Ecological camp, has written extensively about the traditional wisdom of indigenous peoples, including Native Americans. Deep Ecology transcends short-term political demands and asks us to question many of the values underlying western culture in its present phase.

The spiritual evolution represented by Deep Ecology is a move away from doctrinaire theory, the use of force (physical or psychic) and the illusion of human dominance. It is a movement towards non-violence and the partnership between humanity and all other beings, or as the Jains call it, Jiva Daya: the identification with all of life. The struggle to live more lightly is identical with the struggle to uncover the true self. The reduction of carbon is part of the reduction of karma.

How Karma Works

In the Jain dharma, there is no First Cause, divine creator or Supreme Being. Life energy is pervasive and life arises spontaneously – and becomes karmically embodied – for no apparent reason. Time, the earth and the universe are cyclical and self-renewing. And so, although the purpose of each life form, as it comes into existence, is to realize itself and achieve as much spiritual growth as possible, the underlying *why* remains unanswered. This perspective is Many-Sided, for it allows for multiple possible explanations, none of which are more 'correct' than another. At the same time, it shows a realistic awareness of the limits of human knowledge, for a sense of our limitations, as well as our potential, is a key to spiritual progress. And because it has intrinsic value, life does not in any case need a 'reason' to exist and does not need to justify itself to a higher power. Instead, life forms arise into existence spontaneously. In so doing, they are born into enlightenment but are also instantly mired in karma. Their purpose then becomes the quest for knowledge, rational and intuitive, which will enable them to loosen their karmic bonds and then release themselves from samsara, the cycle of mundane existence and rebirth.

Karma is conceived as matter, albeit subtle matter, which exists outside the level of normal consciousness and can only be perceived by enlightened beings. Because karma is matter – 'actual physical material which makes the soul impure'[17] – its workings are described in material, even mechanistic, terms as much as in metaphysical language. The Jain explanation for the mechanism of karma arises from the 'Nine Reals' (i.e. aspects or levels of reality), or *Tattvas*. These are regarded as underlying principles of how the universe operates. The Tattvas can be summarized as follows:

1. *Jiva*: the soul as a unit of pure consciousness or life monad.
2. *Ajiva*: all that is 'non-soul' or purely material in nature. This includes our gross or 'physical' bodies and the 'identities' we assume, our true identity being the jiva or inner consciousness. Karmic embodiment encases the soul in ajiva, which is a state of false consciousness.
3. *Asrava*: the inflow of karmic particles to the soul, making it lose awareness of its self and its clarity of perception. Asrava is often compared to the leakage of water into a damaged vessel.
4. *Bandha*: 'bondage' of the soul; the process by which karmic particles attach themselves and adhere to the jiva and exercise influence.
5. *Punya*: the principle of auspicious karma. This can be understood as 'good' karma, or positive actions which, although inherently karmic, can point the way towards enlightenment.
6. *Papa*: the principle of inauspicious karma. This can be understood as 'bad' karma, or negative actions which point towards a downward spiral or spiritual regression – or merely inauspicious rebirth and entrapment in the karmic cycle.
7. *Samvara*: the stoppage of karmic inflow. This process eventually counters asrava. It is achieved through heightened awareness, leading to a spiritual and intellectual discipline that eventually repels karmic particles. Samvara is likened to the process of repairing a damaged vessel, so that water no longer seeps in. The damaged vessel in question is the soul or life force.
8. *Nirjara*: the shedding of karmic particles. This can take place through the practice of physical austerities, or *tapas*. It can be

hastened by reducing our dependence on narrowly material preoccupations. There is also a natural process by which karmic particles 'bear fruit' and fall away, since like other aspects of ajiva, they are finite.

9. *Moksha*: spiritual and physical liberation, or freedom from karmic bondage. In attaining Moksha, the true self is realized and pure consciousness is achieved. The jiva is released from the karmic cycle and becomes omniscient. For Jains, this is the ultimate goal of all practice. The concept of practice is much wider than one might expect, encompassing all aspects of lived experience, 'ordinary life' as much as meditation or asceticism.

In the Tattvas, we find a process that can, initially, seem arbitrary and impersonal. Karma, it appears, is random and outside of our control, either as individuals or as a human species. Such qualities are also ascribed to 'nature' by a human culture obsessed with control and with imposing its own vision of reason and order on all around it. This restricted view of reason is, in itself, irrational and its consequences have proved environmentally and socially disastrous. For it is our present dominant world-view that is mechanistic and exclusive of everything that cannot be measured or categorized. As we become aware of the limitations of our 'progressive' thought, we turn towards ancient but enduring systems of spiritual guidance such as karma which, whether we interpret them literally or as metaphor, can enrich our understanding and fill the gaps in our (pseudo-) rational 'knowledge'.

Unlike the various 'progressive' world-views, karma is organic, cyclical and inclusive. It connects all areas of life, and each unique life form, within the inhabited universe. Therefore, when we become aware of karma, we become aware of our relationship to all other life. We understand in more depth our individuality *and* our membership of the community of beings, a membership that overrides all other human-made allegiances. Individual life arises spontaneously, but through the karmic process connects instantly to other lives, with which it interacts as it spiritually evolves. The point of beginning, pure consciousness, is also the point of return, Moksha. Time and the universe are cyclical in form and the energy of life is indestructible.

In the idea of rebirth (which once again we can interpret either precisely or figuratively), we are reminded of our continuity with all other species, not just those with which we have the closest genetic links. In the samsaric cycle, the jiva can incarnate in animal, plant or human form, and so we cannot take human rebirth for granted. The Jain view of evolution is subtler than that which is conventionally accepted in western society, allowing for a zigzag pattern of loss and gain rather than a seemingly inevitable forward march of progress.

Karma is deterministic, in the sense that all life is enmeshed in it. But it also an individual journey in which we are given the possibility of exercising free will, making choices and deciding our future. In karma, there is a reconciliation of principles that to the western mind are usually seen as opposites. Determinism and free will, feeling and reason, spirit and matter are part of the same process. Evolution is a spiritual as much as a genetic process, and includes ethical and moral choice as much as the physical processes of development or regression. Karma breaks through and makes trivial the boundaries we create to delude and reassure ourselves. Yet it also enables us to differentiate between what is important and what is transient and illusory. Thus the karmic critique of materialism finds common cause with the ecological critique of progress and unrestrained growth.

In Jain cosmology, the jiva's quality of pure consciousness is corrupted by the same energy that defines it as life force. As each unit of life comes into existence it moves and its vibrations, or *aura*, attract karmic inflow. Jiva is thereby encased in ajiva, the soul becomes embodied, loses its full consciousness and has to find a way out through many rebirths. Until consciousness is reawakened, the inflow of karmic particles becomes unstoppable. They can be neutral or even auspicious, in which case they will be 'shed' as part of a natural process, but they can also be corrupting – or, as many Jains say, 'polluting', when the wrong choices are made. Five main influences shape the influence of karma:

Mithyatva: one-sided or perverted world-view
Pramada: carelessness or indifference
Avirati: lack of discipline
Yoga: activity
Kasaya: passions

Virati, or self-discipline, by contrast, has a positive effect on karma, helping to block its inflow and reducing its ill-effects. Passions can be overcome or controlled, and not all passions are in themselves negative, although even the most positive ones can tip into destructive mode: love into obsession which ceases to be love, faith into dogma that poisons the whole basis of faith. *Mithyatva,* the one-sided or perverted world-view, leads logically towards Ekant, or extremism. It includes utopian ideologies alongside nihilistic cults, for both distort the minds of their followers and result in suffering. At root, Mithyatva is human arrogance, which spans the spectrum from politically correct self-righteousness to the assertion of human dominance or the supremacy of one human group over others. The practice of equanimity, benevolence towards others (human or non-human) and measured conduct lighten the karmic burden.

Karma attaches itself to the jiva in eight principal ways:

1. *Jnanavarniya karma* – obstructs true knowledge; includes the closing of the mind and the acceptance of prejudiced, one-

sided opinions.

2. *Darsanavarniya karma* – obstructs intuition; includes the denial of the spiritual dimension and the value of insight.

3. *Antaraya karma* – obstructs the flow of positive energy; includes mean-spiritedness, bitterness, cynicism and inability to enjoy life. This karma perpetuates negative patterns of thinking and acting.

4. *Mohaniya karma* – deluding or self-deluding karma. Perhaps the most dangerous type of karma, Mohaniya is associated with the conviction of absolute truth and the desire to impose that 'truth' on others.

5. *Vedaniya karma* – pleasure or pain inducing karma; includes those actions which give pleasure or positive gain to others (*sata-vedaniya*) and those which create unhappiness, pain or violence (*asata-vedaniya*).

6. *Ayus karma* – life-span determining karma; the karma that determines length of life.

7. *Nama karma* – birth and physique determining karma. This includes the species or type of organism in which the soul is embodied.

8. *Gotra karma* – status determining karma; establishes the status of a human birth and the accompanying conditions for spiritual development.

These karmic categories come in two types: *ghatiya* or destructive karma, *aghatiya* or non-destructive karma. The first type, which includes categories 1 to 4, involves active harm; the second, which includes categories 5 to 8, can impede spiritual progress but need not cause active harm, indeed in some cases can do good. Category 5, Vedaniya karma, can point in both directions. Through spiritual – which includes ecological – awareness, we can reduce karmic influences in our present lives and determine future existences.

In the Jain dharma, although exceptions are always admitted, it is assumed that only a human rebirth can create the conditions for spiritual development, and therefore humans must strive to avoid rebirth in another form. This is not because animal (or, for that matter, plant) species are innately inferior or less truly 'alive', but because humans have a greater degree of *manobala*, or critical reasoning. Humans are able to evaluate situations at an intellectual as well as purely instinctive or intuitive level, to express themselves in language and abstract thought, to speculate and see beyond their immediate self-interests. These factors give them a greater innate capacity for spiritual development. They have the ability to choose to modify their actions, restrain their behavior and think through the ethical implications of everything they do – or, just as importantly, refrain from doing.

None of this is intended to assert that humans alone have the capacity for reasoning, language or ethical judgment. From both Jain and ecological standpoints, the abilities and potential wisdom of all species are celebrated, an insight borne out increasingly by scientific evidence. Yet it must be acknowledged that humans have by far the strongest deliberate impact on the planet and have some unique abilities to reason or experience spiritual insight. These abilities give us responsibilities – to be careful in our actions, to exercise compassion and be aware of the effects, immediate and long-term, of any act we undertake. Thus human responsibilities more than balance any rights we might claim on grounds of intelligence and creativity. Such rights do not extend to exploiting or oppressing others for our own ends, for in so doing we invariably injure ourselves.

From this it follows that the human capacity to generate destructive karma is far greater than that of any other species or organism. Humans can reach great heights of spiritual development and even escape the cycle of samsara. But the same abilities allow us to fall far further and express the lowest and most negative forms of consciousness. At the individual level, this leads to inauspicious or regressive rebirth, at the collective level to the corruption and death of human civilizations – for which the system of cyclical time allows. The Jain view of karma reminds us that human intelligence does not give us the right to exercise power. Or, put another way, it enables us to see through superficial or destructive forms of power and find real power in the exercise of restraint.

The Greening of Karma

Our karmic entanglement is perpetuated by a confusion of jiva with ajiva, that which is real with that which is false, that which is permanent with that which is transient. In the same way, our loss of ecological balance arises from our sacrifice of long-term needs for instant gratification. A delusion of grandeur that is identical with Mohaniya, the deluding karma of Jainism, has led to the use of our human creative power as an instrument of domination. We have behaved as if the rest of the natural world were simultaneously apart from us and belonging to us, for our continuous use, in all circumstances, without needs, feelings, rights or value aside from that which we arbitrarily assign.

Ecological consciousness and karmic awareness both remind us that we are embedded in and dependent on the rest of nature. We are continuous with all other life, not above or beyond. Within the Jain dharma, all forms of life have value in themselves because they possess jiva and so have the potential to attain enlightenment. Ecological consciousness recognizes the inherent value of all life because of the connections between all life forms which, whether obvious or hidden, make all life forms indispensable parts of a larger process. We are aware that even the smallest or subtlest disruption of or damage to an ecosystem can disrupt or damage the whole of life on earth. That includes human life, for our delusion of a human-versus-nature, civilized-versus-wild barrier leaves us vulnerable to natural forces which we have ceased to understand, experience or feel.

To ecological and karmic consciousness alike, the value of a life form is intrinsic and independent of its supposed 'usefulness' to humanity, or susceptibility to human exploitation. The term 'life' is comprehensive, for it includes rivers, landscapes, mountains and rock formations because these contain and nurture life. In the Jain universe, after all, even the tiniest particles, invisible to the naked eye, are owed protection because of their value and importance. This principle governs the whole of the Jains' way of life and the way they view the world around them.

In similar vein, karmic awareness and ecological consciousness are both founded on respect for the diversity of life. This diversity is inherently worthwhile and it also holds up a model for human society, which becomes distorted when it fails to recognize diversity of culture and species, and beyond that diversity the unique worth of each individual life. According to the platform of Deep Ecology drawn up by Arne Naess and American philosopher George Sessions, humans have no right to reduce the richness and diversity of life 'except to satisfy vital needs'.[18] Jain dharma is a process of questioning our definition of need, so that we learn to consume less and give reduction of harm priority over temporary fulfillment.

Lasting fulfillment arises from living within limits and re-evaluating priorities in terms of creative pursuits and co-operation rather than material accumulation and competition for finite resources. The psychological and social damage caused by the 'long hours' culture is increasingly recognized as meaningless, with much of the work and stress involved lacking in value or even positively harmful. The culture of unfulfilling work is sustained by the addiction to materialism, just as the despoliation of the environment is the product of our addiction to economic growth.

For ecologists, the principal ideological change is crisply defined by Naess as 'that of appreciating life quality (dwelling in situations of inherent value) rather than adhering to an increasingly high standard of living'.[19] This ideological change has nothing to do with the outmoded concepts of 'left' and 'right', but it is required to sustain a change in behavior and break the addiction to growth.

In Jain dharma, material accumulation is matched by karmic accumulation, therefore leading a simpler outward life is the way to see more clearly and cultivate the life within. An understanding of both karmic and ecological processes confirms for us that present human interference with the non-human world has reached the level of collective mania.

We have let ourselves get caught in a destructive cycle. The way out of that cycle involves learning to appreciate the difference between 'bigness' and 'greatness', the distinction between materialistic power and spiritual strength. Jainism is, ultimately, other-worldly in that the ultimate goal of pure consciousness is no longer rooted on earth. The liberated soul is, in this sense, no longer interconnected like the embodied jiva but exists entirely in its own right. Yet in walking, ever more carefully, on the path to this goal, the Jain adept is conscious of a connection to all the diversity of life and a responsibility to use human intelligence to nurture, protect and sustain life.

In both approaches, green and karmic, the relationship between unsustainable patterns of living and exploitative human relationships is highlighted. Jainism is the expression of some of the earliest spiritual insights of the human race, but it acquired its distinctive present form from repudiating practices of discrimination and dominance.

Mahavira specifically challenged the idea that only male members of the Brahmin caste were advanced enough to receive spiritual knowledge, restating the ancient Indic principle that knowledge was available to all – to women as well as men, to rich and poor alike, to people of all stations in life and all ways in life because we are all on the same journey and need to live according to the same principles.

Moreover, unequal divisions of caste (or race and sex) are harmful in themselves because they create hierarchies of dominance. With these come attitudes of arrogance, contempt and prejudice from the dominant, resentment, anger and pain from the dominated. Both oppressed and oppressors experience fear, and fear leads to violence of thought and action. Exploitative relationships are a powerful barrier to perception. As such, it is the duty of the spiritually aware man or woman to work to dismantle them at the social level, and to avoid exploitation or violence in the private sphere. For Jains, the connection between the exploitation of animals and the exploitation of humans is obvious, although it is a connection that most enlightened western liberals find hard to grasp. Factory farms and dehumanized urban housing both lie on a continuum of karmic delusion. They are not separate 'issues' that can be conveniently compartmentalised, but aspects of the same ethical distortion.

Jains are immediately conscious of the links between environmental destruction and neurosis, illusions of human dominance over nature, or the illusion that one human group should dominate another on grounds of race, color, class or caste.

Such false consciousness propels territorial aggression to gain control of people and 'resources', with both humans and non-humans reduced to economic units rather than beings with minds and spirits. The illusion of dominance arises out of the confusion of jiva with ajiva, which leads to the outward assertion of power, rather than the conquest of the self within. True heroism – and we recall that Mahavira's name means Great Hero – is a turning from relationships of dominance, exploitation and greed, and a repudiation of one-sided ideologies that give them sustenance.

Respect for diversity within humanity and nature ensures that the principle of equality is applied with compassion and under-standing. For equality does not require that every person, every thing, be treated as if they were identical rather than unique and varied. Nor does it mean that individuals, human or non-human, are lumped crudely into groups based on supposed identity and allegedly common interests or need. Both the Jain and the ecological approaches base their concepts of equality on an acknowledgement of difference and a celebration of its value. In Jainism, each unit of life is unique and has the potential for self-realization. All life must therefore be accordingly honored, all differences met with acceptance and tolerance.

The ecological movement has arisen out of a revolt against monoculture, a realization at intellectual and intuitive levels that the attempt to induce uniformity is destroying something within the human psyche as well as poisoning the planet. Thus it becomes possible to avoid the flaw that ultimately destroys so many movements for emancipation – the confusion of individual and group identity in which the former is suppressed to serve the latter. A narrow, reactionary view of individual autonomy is equally avoided. There is such a thing as a society and it extends far beyond the human realm. Our individuality is enhanced and fulfilled by our sense of connection with others.

Ecologists whose perspective is spiritual are accused by other environmental campaigners of being overly concerned with the inner life. Therefore, it is alleged that they are not concerned enough with the here-and-now. Such criticisms come, in the main, from those whose energies are focused entirely on single-issue campaigns, such as opposition to a planned housing scheme, the cause of animal welfare or the protection of rainforests. These campaigns are good and valuable in themselves, but often the activists involved cannot see the wood for the trees. They fail to make connections between the campaigns, or to realize the importance of a wider change in the way we think about politics.

Criticism also comes, at times quite stridently, from those who see 'the environment' as but one issue in a collection of causes or part of a wider movement for change – the green stripe in a 'progressive' rainbow coalition. In general these criticisms misunderstand Deep Ecology, which is as interested as the 'left' in social transformation and global justice, and accepts the value of single-issue campaigns. The difference is that the environment is the first cause, out of which all other issues flow and into which they feed back. Without ecological justice there can be no social justice, without a shift from economic expansion to quality of life, the problems of poverty and inequality can never be adequately addressed.

In political ecology, unlike more conventional movements, the individual conscience is the beginning, instead of the mass consciousness. Karmic awareness also starts with the individual. The shedding of layers of karma runs parallel to the removal of layers of warped political and economic priorities, associated with domination and expansion. Karmic awareness is the ecology of the soul. Green consciousness is the spiritual dimension of politics. From their spiritual and political standpoints, they direct us towards social justice and economic democracy in place of exploitation and inequality, towards co-operation rather than competition and fear. Without such changes in relationships between human beings, there can be no spiritual liberation, personal fulfillment or ecological balance.

Karma, Many-Sidedness and Politics

According to Mahavira, karma even has color. There are six *lesyas*, or karmic colorations: *krishna* (black), *neel* (blue), *kapota* (grey), *tejo* (red or sometimes yellow), *padma* (pink) and *sukla* (white). The subtle body, influenced by karma, fluctuates continuously between these shades of color, which fade into each other and overlap at all points on the spectrum between the 'black' and 'white' souls. At the moment of transmigration, the color of the karmic matter indicates the health of the soul and so has a bearing on its next embodiment.

Karmic colors can be experienced by the spiritually attuned, and in a curious form of spiritual synaesthesia can be smelled and tasted as well as being visible at the subtle level. Color is symbolic of mood and moral state in eastern as well as western thought, and in the context of karmic matter white occupies the virtuous end of the karmic spectrum, but freedom from karma is associated with pristine clarity, the total absence of lesyas.

Jains also liken the karmic process to the effects on a crystal of discoloration. The crystal is the jiva, or soul, which in its pure state is luminous and transparent. But contamination with dirt, or being held against backgrounds of various colors, makes it lose that clarity. When the crystal is restored to its original clear, colorless light, this symbolizes release from karmic influence.

The image of the crystal is also one of the most important representations of Anekant. The crystal has many facets, through all of which the same light is reflected. This is one of many illustrations of the idea that the same truth can be reached from many different paths and viewed from many different angles. Error occurs when the angle through which the light is viewed is confused with the light itself, when the path is confused with the summit and the partial is confused with the whole. When one becomes uncritically attached to a particular path, and closes off all other possibilities, that path loses any of its truth and becomes a delusion.

Attachment to ideas can generate negative karma, both because thought *is* action in Jainism and because such attachments lead inexorably to harmful acts. The one-sided viewpoint is associated with the karma of delusion, Mohaniya, for it is a delusion of intellectual grandeur and privileged access to the truth. The greater our certainty, the further we are from enlightenment. A one-sided perspective is the basis of Mithyatva, the perverted worldview, which in turn generates new layers of karma. One-sidedness is a form of attachment, and attachment is the root of karmic activity. Therefore the reduction of karma is associated with the letting go of ideological along with material attachments. Enlightenment is identified with Many-Sidedness, and the spiritual quest is presented as a journey away from dogma rather than the blind embrace of absolute 'truths' that become mere distortions of reality.

It is at this point that we can grasp the relevance of karma and Many-Sidedness to modern politics. An ancient and, to many, abstruse idea can seem less than relevant to the concerns we face. When we look more closely, we are likely to find that many of the most acute political and social problems stem from attachment, whether to ideology, wealth or the various illusions of dominance. One-sided viewpoints are the motivating forces of aggression, including terrorism and war, inequitable distribution of wealth, along with the pollution and destruction of the planet.

Globally and locally, the adversarial nature of politics accentuates these divisions. It promotes a climate of one-sidedness when complex and multi-faceted approaches are required. In this context, it is the ideologies of progress and certainty that have failed, because they erect artificial divisions between human groups, between humanity and the rest of existence, and between individual and collective. They create disconnectedness and perpetuate attachments. The emergence of a politics of Many-Sidedness therefore depends on our letting go of old certainties, a category which includes the apparently 'new' and radical, which is as damaging as the reactionary and narrow when it is empowered by the same dogmatic certainty.

Letting go – or, as Arne Naess has called it, 'the slogan of "non-interference"'– might seem an inadequate solution to pressing and devastating problems, many of which surely cry out for more intervention rather than less. Yet to assume a division between letting go and intervening is to lapse into either/or thinking. Letting go is the starting point, rather than the end in itself, because it creates the conditions for clarity thinking. When we let go of ideas of dominance, or even ideals of perfection, we are better able to decide when and how to intervene, and above all be clear about our motives for so doing.

The spiritual message of karma is that it is the light touch rather than the attempt to control that enables enlightenment to take place. The political message of ecology is that the balance between human beings and the planet is restored by restraint – by 'living as if nature mattered'. That is not a retreat from social activism. On the contrary, it is the beginning of a different type of activism, based on the non-violence of the mind.

Chapter 5

Growing Beyond 'Growth'

Jainism does not fortify its followers by the terrors of karma,
nor does it make them languish in unhealthy, effeminate fatalism,
as many people think all Oriental religions do, but on the contrary,
it trains the individual to become a true hero on the
battlefield of self-conquest.
Charlotte Crause,
The Heritage of the Last Arhat Mahavira (1930)[20]

The Revolution Within

This extraordinary and gloriously politically incorrect insight by
a western Indologist should be seen in the context of its time. The
theme it touches upon is more timeless, doing much to explain
the lasting appeal of Jainism, and why it is relevant to us at this
point in our civilization's history. The 'us' in question is western
societies, certainly, but also the emerging global community,
where western attitudes towards economics and politics prevail,
often presented as 'the only game in town'.

One-sided thinking has focused on the projection of ideas,
through persuasion or by force, from one individual or human
group to another. This principle applies to much of organized
observance, mass education, economics, political debate,
militarism and territorial expansion. Enlightenment is equated
with 'winning the argument', acquiring the greatest number of
followers, economic growth and the conquest of territory (which
becomes 'ours' rather than 'theirs'). Political discussion is a
'battle of ideas' rather than a search for greater knowledge or
closeness to the truth. It is about the dominance of one idea over

another rather than shared values or common dreams. Human hierarchies are founded on one-sided ideologies of dominance and control. These in turn are rooted in the idea of human rule over nature, the innate supremacy and special qualities of humankind. Nature has been 'conquered' and made an instrument of perpetual human power, because humanity is uniquely intelligent and creative. All systems of human dominance – racial, social and economic or sexual – derive from this first principle of one-sidedness.

Stripped to their bare essentials, the principles of one-sidedness seem naïve, almost innocent, were their consequences not so destructive. Yet they retain a powerful hold over the mind, which is akin to, indeed a product of, the system of karmic bondage, which blocks our awareness of reality. The search for Many-Sided truth is therefore also a quest for equanimity. But that is not the same as neutrality or disengagement. It is clarity of vision, uncluttered by attachments, whether material or doctrinaire.

The Jains of Mahavira's day understood this. They recognized that the notion of a hierarchy of species, based on power, was as false as parallel hierarchies among human beings. They realized that uncritical submission to gurus, teachers or political leaders led to collective delusions, which led in turn to oppression and violence. Therefore, they accepted that each man and woman is his or her own guru, and that spiritual development is the responsibility of the individual, that spiritual teachers can only guide, rather than impose their will on others. They also realized that reason loses its rational essence if it denies the spiritual component of the universe and blinds us to the interconnectedness of all life.

All this points towards a new approach to human reason, society and spiritual practice. Or rather, not a new approach, but the revival of ancient, intuitive wisdom to enrich and complement modern knowledge. These impulses also inform much of New Age thinking and practice in our contemporary western world. There is the same rejection of hierarchy and over-organization, especially in the religious sphere. 'I reject organized religion', 'I am spiritual but not religious' are watch-words of New Age practice. They would have been recognized by Mahavira and his followers – except that the questions raised by the New Age are too often only superficially answered, which is far worse than no answer at all. There is the same questioning of the prevailing assumptions about material progress, with a search for something more profound, a vaguely defined new source of wisdom. There is the same search for a balance between reason and intuition, spirituality and science. R.D. Laing, the radical psychiatrist, expressed this sense very clearly when he asked: 'How can we be so superstitious as to suppose the soul does not exist because we cannot see it at the end of a micro-scope?'

The green movement has also arisen out of a questioning of our individual and collective priorities, in particular our obsession with consumption and our equation of material over-abundance with human happiness. Frustration with the growth-oriented politics of right and left, and awareness that the earth's resources are finite rather than limitless, have both given impetus to green political expression. Such awareness is expressed variously through systematic party programs, a series of single issue campaigns or attempts to exert a lobbying influence on conventional – 'grey' – politics. Green consciousness stems from advances in the science of ecology, which make us aware of previ-ously hidden connections between the diverse life forms of the earth. Science also makes us aware that humans are not as different from other species as we have often arrogantly assumed. Furthermore, the illusion of difference is destroying our environment and threatening both our lives and the material progress we extol. The green movement is supposed to be about re-examining our relationship with nature, as much as with each other, and challenging previously fixed attitudes towards progress and power. It also offers the possibility of an overlap between the scientific, spiritual and political processes.

New Age spirituality and green politics both have the same starting points as Jain philosophy and Jain practice, then and now. The difference is that the first two movements, as products of the western industrial civilization they overtly challenge, reflect its values and prejudices. This problem does much to account for the hedonistic, commercialized element in the New Age, which is pervasive and now often proudly celebrated as proof of 'success'. Equally, it explains why the green movement has become partisan and one-sided and has in practice failed to reach beyond the right/left, either/or adversarial structure of modern politics. Adversarialism has become its karmic entanglement, raising its short-term profile but undermining or diluting its original purpose.

The main difference between New Age thinking and the path of Many-Sidedness lies in the definition of self, and self-fulfillment. While opposition to materialism and conformity are central to New Age thought, the impulse to self-fulfillment is itself materialistic. More often than not, it is conformist as well, because it requires uncritical acceptance of attitudes and tastes more rigid than those of the rejected 'mainstream'. Self-fulfillment is identified with the enactment of desire and the absence of restraint, external or internal. Furthermore, it is equated with a one-sided rejectionism, a hangover from the rejection of 'bourgeois values' of the revolutionary (but not truly radical) left.

With rejectionism comes self-righteousness and a complacent assumption of being nearer to the truth or on a higher spiritual path than others. This is the opposite of Many-Sidedness, which is based on humility in the face of truth. 'Right Knowledge' only emerges when we become aware of our ignorance and our limits. The New Age, by contrast, tends to question any idea of limits.

105

This approach is a continuation of human arrogance by other means. Dangerously, it confuses the superficial self with the true self. Fulfillment arises through a form of spiritual consumerism and pick-and-mix morality, with inconvenient ideas or practices ignored or denounced in the name of modernization or western 'liberal' values.

Spiritual consumerism usually turns out to be as much a dead end as the overtly material consumption culture which it opposes, but of which it is really an offshoot. The New Age rejection of 'mainstream' or 'middle-class' values is a largely negative phenomenon, based on anger and frustration rather than clarity of perception, and despite the pretence of egalitarianism is sneeringly elitist in practice. Based on the one-sided principle of classifying and dismissing others, it ignores both the complexity and uniqueness of each individual, and the shared values that hold communities together.

The same element of self-righteousness has crept into much of green campaigning and politics. For this reason, a vehicle for possible social transformation has turned into a movement of perpetual opposition, based on intemperate anger rather than calm reflection and an examination of issues from the roots upwards. In place of a questioning of one's own values and priorities, and encouraging others to do the same, the emphasis is on condemning and criticizing, on being 'against' rather than 'for'.

This stance is counter-productive for two reasons. First, it alienates many of those who would be attracted to the idea of living more simply and abandoning attachments. It gives them the impression that green values are punitive and puritanical, instead of life-affirming, and so plays into the hands of those who most fear and resist a change of consciousness. Secondly, it undermines both the work and the underlying thinking of green campaigners themselves, limiting their ability to reach out to opponents or skeptics or to break the negative pattern of either/or thinking that is the basis of the ecological crisis itself.

In other words, the New Age often resembles a marketing niche within the consumer society it set out to challenge. The green movement, meanwhile, has become part of the political and cultural ghetto of the left, with the accompanying righteous anger and destructive rage. As a spiritual movement, the New Age succumbs to a shallow view of the self, based on gratification of immediate desires and transient emotional needs. In its political expression, the green movement divides human beings into categories of 'right' and 'wrong' (or left and right) and balkanizes them into 'communities' based on race, faith or gender rather than shared human qualities and shared human problems.

Yet both movements are expressions of something valuable that is as much a part of what we call 'human nature' as delusions of grandeur or attachment to material possessions and power. They arise from a search for healing and wholeness, a sense that something is profoundly wrong with the way our society is organized, because of the distorted perceptions that we carry with us, individually and collectively. The two movements, one spiritual and inner-directed, the other political and social, ask profound questions but frequently provide only superficial answers. Or, to put it another way, they provide no answers at all because they keep us locked into patterns of thought that derive from separation and conflict. They question everything except the way we think. They have yet to learn that the way we form our opinions is as important as the opinions themselves, just as intent is as important as action.

The New Age view of the self is based on narrow individualism – the self as consumer in search of liberation through fulfillment. The green-left view of the self is based on narrow collectivism – the self as part of a rigidly defined 'community', in search of liberation through a 'progressive coalition' of 'communities'. Both views closely resemble each other, even though they seem at first glance to be opposites. For the consumerist self is as incomplete, and deluded, as the politicized self that follows a 'correct' line and relies on simplistic divisions between human beings. Both lack the Many-Sided perspective that sees the self as at once unique and continuous.

Many-Sidedness is derived from a holistic view of the self. Each individual, each living organism, is unique and distinctive, containing its own truth. But that truth is part of a larger truth, in the same way as that self is part of a much larger process. It is a unit of life, but connected to all other life forms through both the evolutionary process and the spiritual journey. The 'self' is affected by a series of accumulated experiences that cross the boundaries of species as well as race or gender. These experiences might not be confined to earthly incarnation. The four Gati (destinies) of Jainism include rebirth in an unworldly or extra-terrestrial form, as well as the more familiar categories of human, animal or plant. No two 'selves' are identical. Each is at a different point in the karmic cycle, in the same way as each is at a different point in the journey towards truth, from blinkered vision to clarity of vision. But the self transcends the human person and the individual life span.

It follows that the idea of self-realization involves putting the immediate, superficial concerns of the self into perspective. That perspective is at once global, human and universal. For it takes account of the accumulated experience of the self, transforming it into wisdom and clear-sightedness. It is grounded in the connection between the self and all other forms of life, the awareness that all life is interconnected and so violence against one life is violence against all – and violence against the self. You *are* that which you injure, oppress or abuse because the same life force pervades and activates all beings. And inevitably, a sense of the vastness of time and its continuous repetitive cycles, upwards and downwards, gives us a perspective on our concerns, a sense of humility and awe. But self-realization is also a turning within and a realizing of hidden powers. It is a peeling away of layers of conditioning, and learning to think in a new way, clearing the mind of violent thoughts, not just because they are violent but because they are uncreative products of attachment. By knowing our limitations, we can begin to realize our potential.

A Many-Sided perspective allows us to move beyond the consumerist obsessions of much of the New Age movement. Or, expressed more positively, it allows the New Age movement to return to its original goal. That is the reawakening of the human spirit in its true sense, rather than the one-dimensional 'achievements' of human supremacism, which have wounded us at least as much as they have advanced us.

The green movement can also retrieve its founding purpose of reconnecting humanity with nature and human beings with themselves, and of breaking the artificial barriers of either/or, right and left. That perspective could give authority and vision to campaigns for social or environmental justice, rather than relegating them to a ghetto of one-sided militancy. In place of the fabricated 'communities' of identity politics, the true community encompasses all living beings that have the capacity for spiritual development.

Anekant creates a deeper shade of green and introduces to the New Age something genuinely new, which is also an ancient wisdom. This means doing more than attempting to change one's behavior and requiring others to change. The real challenge lies in changing the thought patterns that affect and influence behavior, learning to think in inclusive circles rather than straight, exclusive lines. It means more than admitting that the earth's resources are finite, as today's ecological imperative demands. Admitting that human intelligence is also a finite resource, because it is inherently limited, helps us to understand the need to live within limits. More importantly, it liberates us from the constraints associated with human supremacism, which creates a siege mentality in humanity's relationship with the rest of nature.

According to the supremacist model, humanity must always

'conquer', 'triumph' or 'master' and this produces a relationship with nature based ultimately on fear, like the fears that underlie attempts by one race or one gender to dominate another. Knowing the limits of human intelligence liberates us from that siege mentality and enables us to use our intelligence in creative ways. Just as acceptance of finite resources allows us to live more fulfilling lives, so acceptance of our limits as a species enables us to fulfill our potential, instead of closing off large areas of experience.

Although Anekant starts from the perspective of admitting human limits, it is about pursuing knowledge and acquiring as much wisdom as possible. The concept of knowledge is expansive and includes what is now described – especially in New Age circles – as emotional intelligence. This means the ability to empathize with other humans and all beings, to understand other ways of looking at the world and make the protection and continuity of life the basis for all decisions. In this sense, empathy is an aspect of Many-Sidedness. It is part of the process of letting go of ideas of dominating and exploiting others.

Human intelligence comes into its own in helping us let go of such ideas, and developing more co-operative ways of living. Dietary choices, for instance, can be guided by human intelligence. Reducing our consumption of meat is a conscious human choice for planetary and human health, and for breaking the pattern of exploitation of animals. Mass addiction to continuous meat eating leads to cruel and inhuman factory farms at one level, and world hunger at another. Global demand outstrips supply, and in the materially affluent (but spiritually impoverished) regions of the world, animal welfare is sacrificed before immediate human need. Dietary modification is also an expression of the spiritual link between humanity and other species and the understanding that all life is connected and has a common purpose. The presence of the spiritual is central to Anekant, for the human journey is ultimately a spiritual journey, putting material cravings into perspective.

The strength of human intelligence is that it enables us to discern true needs and favor them over transient desires. This can be said to place humans at an advantage over other life forms. Yet it also imposes an immense burden of responsibility to discriminate between true and false values, potential and limits. Failure to recognize those limits has disastrous consequences for human communities, the ecosystems that sustain life and, above all, the human individual, the self. Real use of human intelligence starts with acknowledging limits. Through this process, we realize our potential as human beings and our ability to co-operate with each other. Likewise, with Anekant, we clear our minds of any dogmatic assumption that we possess superior truths and open ourselves to other possibilities and viewpoints. In so doing, we grow nearer to the truth which we are all trying to grasp in our own ways.

Anekant is a tool for the self-conquest which is the explicit purpose of Jainism, and central to all spiritual practice. Self-conquest is the peeling away of layers of delusional thinking, chiefly delusions of grandeur and power. It is conquest of the very idea of conquest, in the sense of imposing our ideologies on others by force or threats, or assuming that other peoples or creatures exist exclusively for our benefit, as instruments of our power. Such 'conquest' is in reality an outward projection of Ekant, one-sidedness. It is at once a form of self-indulgence and self-harm, for it is the root cause of the social and environmental instability we now face, when our very viability as a species is called into question.

The conquest of self, by contrast, is about dispelling any notion of power over others that can be exerted by force, to the point of consciously opting out of power structures and coercive frameworks. It is about ceasing to feel 'superior' to fellow humans for arbitrary reasons such as race, culture, qualifications or (apparent) differences of intelligence and skill. Equally, it means casting off the assumption of superiority to fellow creatures and acknowledging that they do not exist for us to exploit, but have individual souls and are part of the diversity of life, as much as we are. Spiritual insights are not exclusively human, any more than they are exclusively expressed through language. And western scientific insight is showing us what the ancients already knew: that the differences between humans and other species, although real, are small and not as radical as we pretend.

Self-conquest means being aware of how small we are within the context of the cosmos, but how large the human spirit can become, if we let it evolve. The starting point is the self, the jiva which represents the continuity of life, transcending divisions between species or any of the divisions and differences between human groups. By focusing on the jiva, we abolish the distinction, dominant in the west, between self and other. We realize that all life is intertwined and mutually dependent. By abolishing that division between self and other, we become aware that our value systems are inherently limited and incomplete. And so we surrender all assumptions that we are closer to the truth than others, without surrendering the idea of truth as something to work towards. We become closer to our true selves, because we understand that self has nothing to do with material ambitions or the desire for power over others.

Anekant is an idea specific to Jainism, but it is also a universal goal, with relevance to practitioners of all other faiths or secular ideologies. The practice of Many-Sidedness begins with acceptance of the need for humility, which is prized by all spiritual traditions. When religion and spirituality have taken wrong turnings, it is because they have abandoned that principle. Fundamentalism is based on lack of humility, which leads in turn to repression and violence of all forms. The same is true of secular ideologies. We can see this if we contrast the success of co-operative enterprises in the west or the kibbutz movement in

Israel with the totalitarian incompetence of the Communist world. It is not the idea of common ownership that is wrong in itself, but the attempt by an elite to impose its own vision of society on an unwilling populace. Similarly, the attempt to impose 'democratic' structures from the top downwards, without regard to local conditions or cultural inheritance, leads almost invariably towards corruption and conflict. Scientific reason congeals into narrow-minded dogma when it becomes self-regarding and absolutist. One-sidedness is intellectual violence, which transforms itself into physical violence through the absence both of humility and critical reasoning, the loss of curiosity and the sense of wonder.

The practice of Many-Sidedness begins with letting go. This applies to narrow ideological certainties, delusions of intellectual grandeur and the desire to project power outwards rather than focusing on the power within. Letting go means giving up worldly attachments and being aware of the need to consume less. There is an intimate link between Anekant and a more ecological way of living, which is based on quality rather than quantity. That is the revolution for our times, a process of inner change rather than the imposition of an abstract ideal by force.

Less is More

> *The skilled walker leaves no tracks*
> Laozi (Lao Tse)

Jains are best known to the world for the austere lives of their ascetics. These men and women separate themselves from mainstream society with its conventional standards of behavior, its obligations and attachments. They lead lives of subsistence, calling to mind those indigenous peoples who live closest to nature. In Jain ascetic practice, the memory of an archaic, pre-agrarian way of life is kept alive and combined with reasoned understanding of the universe and an ecological consciousness derived from science as much as intuition. Ascetic Jains remind us, in one sense, of humanity in its purest form, unencumbered by material wants or the trappings of modern life that make us fearful of nature and unable to withstand the elements.

Yet the greatest challenge presented by the ascetics to modern society is their use of human powers of reason to avoid harm to other creatures, or reduce it to the barest minimum. In this respect, their lives are simultaneously primitive and highly advanced. They show that human intelligence can be used to minimize human impact on the earth's ecosystems, rather than expanding human influence and exercising control over others – influence that they know will be counter-productive and control that they know will disintegrate. Ascetics exercise true power and, having conquered themselves, come closer to the reality of the self than any lay people can manage. This is why even (or perhaps especially) wealthy lay Jains envy those who are called to be ascetics and hope that they will eventually reach that level of consciousness.

The lives of ascetic men and women stem from a depth of spiritual commitment that is hard for most to conceive of, let alone experience. In taking the vows of their faith to a logical conclusion, they are also acting out those vows, serving as mentors and guides. They do not demonstrate how everyone should be compelled to live, for the ascetic path does not suit everyone, nor should it. Instead, they embody the principles of Ahimsa and Careful Action. Ascetics provide lay men and women with a yardstick against which to measure their spiritual progress. More than that, these spiritual warriors enable us, as civilians, to put our attachments, commitments and desires into perspective and remember that there are larger goals, based on the ultimate simplicity.

Those who find their way of life threatening, or who view them through prejudiced eyes, see Jain ascetics as life-denying fanatics and fundamentalists. By western, secular standards, they are fanatical, because they abjure the comforts that could be theirs and refuse conventional responsibilities. They can be seen as life-denying as well, because all the priorities and so many of the pleasures of ordinary life are avoided. But the lives of ascetics are more life-affirming than ours, since they are built around the preservation of life and the avoidance of injury. More importantly, perhaps, ascetics are acting out the principle at the heart of Many-Sidedness – the ability to let go.

Initially, this might seem paradoxical. The ascetic way of life is, after all, an absolutist rendering of the principle of non-absolutism. But this reaction is itself a product of either/or thinking. It is falsely to equate the practice of Many-Sidedness with a position of extreme relativism in which nothing is true and everything has equal value, and so no value at all. This way of thinking is associated with various currents of post-modernist thinking, which have dethroned some of the certainties and orthodoxies of western thought, only to embrace another form of one-sidedness, as relativism becomes an orthodoxy in itself and every aspect of life is 'deconstructed', whatever its merits.

Anekant is based on the opposite premise of respect for truth as an absolute value. It is based on a sense of awe in the face of truth, a sense that we can only approach it tentatively, that the aspects of truths we grasp can only be used with extreme care and delicacy. Far from being a denial of truth, Anekant is a process of evolution towards it in which all of humanity, and all of life, is engaged. By living out the principles of non-violence and reduced consumption, Jain ascetics are reminding us of unchanging truths which persist through thousands of years of human 'progress', some of which is real and valuable, but much of which is illusory because it makes us claim powers and privileges we do not possess.

Initially, Jain asceticism was intended for internal consumption. That is to say, it was aimed at other Jains, to teach them how they should live, what they should value, or what they should aspire towards themselves or in future lives. Today, communications between peoples have led to the globalization of ideas almost as much as of economics, and to a wider questioning of values within almost all human cultures. We have already observed that Mahatma Gandhi's contact with Jain ideas enabled him to re-examine his Hinduism. He did not renounce the Hindu dharma and become an atheist, or pretend to be a Jain, but he thought more deeply about the real meaning of the Vedas. This led him to advocate a rebalancing of the relationship between men and women within Hindu society, and an end to practices such as 'untouchability' and caste oppression, for these were a corruption of Vedic ideals as well as an insult to human dignity. He also sought to raise the status of non-violence within Hindu practice, recognizing that Ahimsa is the founding principle and underlying strength of Indic thought. The subtle influence of Jain teachings led Gandhi to become a reformer of Hinduism as well as a pioneer of non-violent political resistance. What is good in Hindu practice is to be preserved, because it contributes to a larger spiritual truth. What is corrupt is to be abolished or transformed, because it part of a wider stream of false consciousness. The same principle can be applied to any of humanity's great philosophical teachings, whether of religious or secular origin.

For the west – and those who seek to emulate its way of life – it is also possible to rethink without destroying indiscriminately. The practice of Many-Sidedness involves learning how to discriminate between true and false, rather than non-discrimination and 'value-free' thought and conduct. It is about valuing all that promotes the dignity of the human person and the interconnectedness of all life, whilst rejecting that which is exploitative and harmful to life. Thus a critique of western civilization need not be opposed to reason, nor should it automatically reject the beneficial effects of technological and scientific progress – to cure disease, relieve pain or improve the environment.

From the perspective of Anekant, we should ally ourselves with those aspects of western science that can lead us away from narrow, linear thinking towards a more holistic or spiritual perspective. We must apply reason to our own behavior and our attempts to change the direction of our society. Reason tells us, as much as our intuition or faith, that our lives are all intertwined and that human destiny is bound up with that of the earth and all life upon it. Such understanding does not run contrary to western ideals of individual liberty and human rights, but reinforces them and gives them new life. Individual license and illusions of human supremacy are distortions of the west's ideals, just as caste and gender-based oppression are distortions of Vedic wisdom.

The example of Jain ascetics is therefore as relevant to 'us' as it is to the Jain laity. It is relevant in much the same way as are the lives of indigenous peoples, who live more fully within the rhythms of nature and thus remind us of human and ecological realities. Early contact with Australian Aborigines led Captain James Cook to write of them in these terms:

> Being wholly unacquainted not only with the superfluous but the necessary Conveniences so much sought after in Europe, they are happy in not knowing the use of them. They live in Tranquility which is not disturb'd [sic] by the inequality of Condition; the Earth and sea of their own accord furnishes them all things necessary for life, they covet not Magnificent Houses, Household-stuff etc. ... In short, they seem'd to set no value upon anything we gave them.[21]

This initial approach of compassionate understanding did not last long, as the experience of colonialism led to the systematic destruction of Aboriginal culture, pieces of which are only now being put together two centuries on. The story has been the same the world over for disparate and varied indigenous peoples, such as the Native Americans and Inuit, the Kalahari 'Bushmen' or the Tibetans today.[22] In the case of the 'Bushmen', cultural oppression and dispossession came from black Africans as much as white colonialists. Membership of an 'oppressed group' is no guarantee of enlightened attitudes and hierarchies of oppression are a product of one-sided thinking. The frenzy of the attack on indigenous cultures suggests more than purely economic and territorial reasons. There was perhaps a strong element of fear, both overt and unconsciousness, in the assault on indigenous peoples and cultures. It is possible that these peoples' implicit rejection of the values associated with relentless economic expansionism threatened their conquerors. Despite their apparent power, they feared the hidden powers of the peoples they subjugated and the truths they embodied. The suppression of indigenous peoples was the attempt to suppress an idea. Or rather it was the attempt to suppress any idea opposed to either/or reasoning and the separation of humanity from nature.

Accounts such as Captain Cook's inspired the myth of the 'Noble Savage'. This became part of Jean-Jacques Rousseau's post-Enlightenment critique of contemporary Europe.[23] The idea of a pristine but lost golden age was also a staple of the Romantic movement's opposition to an organized society that suppressed human emotions. Such mythology had a positive effect in some ways, in that it led to a questioning of received wisdom about power and humanity's relationship to nature, although it has rarely led to questions about human supremacy. Yet the Noble Savage idea was flawed in the sense that it emphasized the 'otherness' of indigenous peoples, at once idealizing them and viewing them as primitive or less fully evolved. It was therefore very different from accepting them as equal human beings, who might have insights and skills that industrial society had forgotten but could relearn. It is no coincidence that revival of interest in indigenous cultures has coincided with a questioning of many of our western certainties and an anxiety about our relationship with the environment. Suddenly, the wisdom of human communities who live in close proximity to nature has relevance and resonance for us.

The lives of Jain ascetics, the wandering *sadhus* of the Hindu tradition and the hermit-sages of Daoism in China all call to mind the indigenous world-view, with its sense of connectedness to something greater than mere humanity. As such, they evoke derision and fear as well as distant respect. The fear arises from the challenge they, like indigenous societies, represent to 'mainstream' aspirations or conventional ideas about progress and power. Yet the fear itself can be turned into a positive force, as the beginning of a change of consciousness. Indigenous societies and ascetic communities or individuals ask us implicitly whether we need to be obsessed with consumption and whether we are in reality harming ourselves when we pursue 'progress' uncritically. They question our assumptions about power and remind us of the areas in which we are weak and helpless against elemental forces, the intensity of which we no longer realize. Their message to us is 'think again' and it is a message to which more and more of us are receptive, even if it is not reflected in the existing power structures or political process. And the beginning of this receptiveness is a rising awareness that less is more, a profound dissatisfaction beneath the relentless consumption. There is a search for something more meaningful beneath the emphasis on brands, possessions and wealth as the only desirable goal and source of security.

'Less is more' is the basis for Aparigraha, the Jain vow of non-possessiveness. Non-possessiveness is an aspect of non-violence, because the desire to possess people, places and objects is the wellspring of violent thoughts and actions. Aparigraha stems from an awareness of the connection between materialism and neurosis. Material cravings become a form of addiction and a death-within-life. A society based on material cravings displays all the irrational, compulsive behaviors of the addict. Those men and women who take the Mahavratas, the Greater Vows of asceticism, practice Aparigraha in the most literal way. They renounce all possessions: in the case of the male Digambaras, this extends even to clothes. Lay Jains, who take the Anuvratas or Lesser Vows, might be materially wealthy, especially in relative terms. Yet they are asked to consider constantly what they really do need and what they could well do without. This lesson is as useful to the rest of the human community. Reducing our ecological footprint is a spiritual goal as much as it is a practical attempt to address the environmental turmoil threatening our lives.

Counter-Power

Nobody is expected to become an ascetic, if that is not their calling, just as nobody is expected to pretend to be 'indigenous' and disavow all of western culture and society. Nor is western society as a whole expected to discard centuries of accumulated technological wisdom and lose its distinctive characteristics. However, the lives of ascetic men and women, like those of surviving indigenous populations, hold up a critical mirror to us. They enable us to question our values and priorities and decide to live our own versions of the Five Vows. While distinctively Jain in their construction, the Vratas embody a primal wisdom that reflects humanity's true nature and our place within nature. They are therefore a resource for the whole of humanity, rather than confined to one faith tradition or geographical area.

Questioning our values is central to the practice of Anekant. Such questioning should not lead to rejection, which is an aspect of one-sidedness. It is an opening towards our civilization's most generous and compassionate characteristics, so that we can use our knowledge in a wise and discriminating manner. Many-Sided questioning is a process of rediscovery, akin to the process by which indigenous peoples, such as the Native Americans and Aborigines, are reclaiming their culture and with it their self-respect. It is a process of re-learning that western culture is not only about destructive competition and the isolation of individuals from one another. Nor is it about the dysfunctional relationship with the earth that mirrors our increasingly fragmented social relationships. A fuller version of individual freedom involves co-operation and a sense of community, with the idea of rights and duties extending beyond the narrow, human realm.

Western science in its present phase is leading us back to a more holistic world-view, in which the spiritual dimension is not dismissed. The linear, mechanistic view of the universe seems suddenly quaint and old-fashioned, rather than 'progressive', and rejection of spirituality is expressed through fundamentalist polemic rather than reasoned argument. In the same way, western political thought needs to make a quantum leap beyond either/or, binary thinking towards Many-Sided thinking, from external to internal growth. We need to find new ways of measuring prosperity, progress and quality of life, less threatening to the planet and ourselves.

In this context, a politics for the New Age must be a process of collective healing, in place of sterile conflict that leads us nowhere. That means a politics of 'less is more', of interconnectedness, a collective process of self-conquest. This is quite different from the familiar politics of conflict, division and ultimately hatred of life. So different, indeed, that many dismiss it as impossible or impractical. A life-affirming politics requires a change of consciousness, an ability to grow beyond the narrow, materialistic definitions of growth, away from adversarial relationships with the environment and fellow humans. It is a politics of counter-power, based on recognition of the true, subtle powers within humanity and nature, rather than the overt manifestations of power, based on delusion and violence. Many-Sidedness is the key to this process. By making us accept human limits, it can unlock human potential.

Chapter 6

A Politics of Many-Sidedness

The end is where we start from
T.S. Eliot, Little Gidding

Neither left nor right but ahead
Founding slogan, German Green Party

Adversarial Karma

Peace is not an absence of war, it is a virtue, a state of mind, a disposition for benevolence, confidence, justice.
Baruch Spinoza

To many, the idea of a politics of Many-Sidedness would seem impossible, a contradiction in terms. This is because politics is surely about winning arguments, about government and opposition, struggles for justice and the defeat of enemies. Disagreement is healthy and necessary, a sign of vigorous democratic life. How then can the idea of Anekant, which is about transcending differences and disagreements, possibly be useful to the political process?

This response misunderstands the nature of Anekant and takes a narrow view of politics. Many-Sidedness does not mean abolishing disagreement. It is a tool of reasoning that can be used by people of all ideological persuasions. Rather than destroying their arguments, it is intended to give them greater depth, subtlety and clarity. More than that, it provides the sense of perspective that prevents ideas from mutating into extremism or solidifying into inflexible dogmas. Many-Sidedness reminds us that we are all engaged in a common human endeavor that overrides political ideology as much as it does faith or ethnicity. This means that Anekant is a potential instrument of healing in the political space, as much as in other areas of human experience. Rather than burying differences, or seeing opponents merely as enemies, it treats different shades of opinion as valuable contributions, from which we can learn and against which we can measure and test our own ideas or assumptions. It also encourages us to view opponents as human beings on a journey to the same place, but working towards it from different points of origin.

Political discussion need not then be a 'battle of ideas', but an encounter between different aspects of the same truth. That involves respect for the dignity and integrity of each individual, even where his or her 'truth' seems very different from one's own, or sometimes abhorrent. This is particularly difficult for those who believe they have truth and justice on their side, or that they are fighting for the rights of oppressed peoples and groups. Understandably, they are unwilling to compromise or make concessions that they see as a sell-out. Yet this attitude of stubborn refusal quickly turns into a position of hatred and intransigence, in which those who work for an apparently just cause acquire some of the worst characteristics of their opponents. The interests they are advancing are thereby diluted, distorted and ultimately destroyed.

The confusion of principle with stubbornness is one of the categorical errors of modern politics, crossing the conventional boundaries of left and right. It is a politics of disconnection, based on an assumption of absolute truth and the impugning or dehumanization of opponents. More than that, the adversarial approach to politics implies a sense of ownership, or at least privileged connection with an idea. At the same time, it turns that idea into an object, existing independently of human control, instead of a product of human experience and imagination. Objects, after all, invite possessive impulses, and so adversarial politics becomes a form of attachment, and so an aspect of the karmic cycle. And so, like other forms of attachment, adversarialism is founded on violent thoughts and actions, and produces more of these. It promotes separation and disconnection, when what is required is a politics of reconnection, in which shared humanity is emphasized above ideological differences, and the concept of social justice extends beyond the satisfaction of immediate human needs.

Open and Closed Ideologies

From the perspective of Many-Sidedness, the main political distinction is less between left and right, or liberal and conservative, as between closed and open, quantitative and qualitative. Closed political ideologies refuse to accept the validity of anything outside their limited world-view and regard those who disagree with them as enemies to be conquered or overthrown. This leads their adherents to dehumanize their opponents, directing violent thoughts and impulses towards them, if not actual violence. Closed ideologies are ideologies of fragmentation. The human individual is either regarded as an isolated unit of production and consumption, or as a nameless, faceless member of a collective grouping that is pitted against other groups. Both approaches are equally reductionist and encourage disconnectedness, rather than trying to arrive at underlying unity. As such, closed ideologies are based on the separation of human beings from each other, and the separation of humanity from the rest of existence. Closed ideologies are human supremacist, interventionist and expansionist at every level. They are therefore inherently violent,

Open ideologies accept that human – and ecological – problems are complex and multi-faceted. Opponents are regarded as full human beings, with all the possibilities and limitations that this implies. Indeed open ideologies are distinguished by their acceptance both of the powers latent in humanity and the limitations of being human. They are also aware of the connections between different areas of policy: between (for example) a well-ordered society at home and the pursuit of peace rather than aggression abroad; social cohesion and a harmonious relationship with the environment; awareness of human diversity and a sense of common purpose.

Closed and open ideologies have a different attitude to power. In closed ideologies, it is expressed overtly and by force. Competing for power is about projecting the loudest voice or having the greatest force of arms. There is a linear progression between these two means of force, and fittingly so, because they are products of linear thinking. Open ideologies, meanwhile, attach more importance to subtle or soft power. They emphasize co-operation and agreement, without abandoning the principles of human dignity and the interconnectedness of life. Open ideologies are about making connections instead of erecting barriers between people and human groups.

The same distinctions exist between expressions of faith. There are closed systems of faith, which are absolutist and brook no opposition to their world-view. There are open forms of spiritual inquiry, in which there is a search for the common roots and goals of spirituality. What is held in common is more important than differences of doctrine and ritual. The first type of spirituality is easily transformed into inflexible fundamentalism, and usually results in the use of force or violence against non-believers and alleged heretics. The aggression is also turned inwards, resulting in unhappiness and trauma for the adherents of a closed system who find themselves torn between its demands and their own more profound needs.

The second, more open form of spirituality is more vulnerable to oppression and 'hard' power, as it is forced into line or stamped out by more rigid orthodoxies. But it has a more subtle strength and a capacity for survival beneath the surface of consciousness. Those who have visited the cathedrals or country churches of England and northern Europe will notice the ancient symbols of fertility and growth, such as the Green Man, carved in wood and stone. As Buddhism spread through Asia, it absorbed local deities and was tolerant and receptive towards local customs. For example, the old religion of Bon exists both within and running parallel to the Tibetan Buddhist tradition. Jainism survived and grew, intellectually and spiritually, within a Hindu majority culture, its followers respecting and sometimes worshipping Vedic gods at the same time as they revered their own Path-Finders.

In the same way, a spirituality of connectedness persists today, as if lying in wait beneath the surface of consciousness. And in an age of rising ecological concern, its time might well have come. The sense that we are in conflict with our environment and need to reconnect with it coincides with a revival of nature-centered spiritualities, from Shinto in Japan to African traditional religions, European paganism and goddess worship to the Daoist interplay of *yin* and *yang*, the natural forces of the universe. Within Christianity, a nature-centered Creation Spirituality and the radically ecological teachings of St Francis of Assisi speak more to our twenty-first century concerns than proscriptive dogmas. Within Islam, the Sufi tradition, which emphasizes the power and gentleness of nature, is in the ascendant, and the esoteric teachings of the Kabbalah, once derided by enlightened Jews, are now studied in depth by Jew and gentile alike. Throughout the world, indigenous peoples find in their most ancient spiritual systems new sources of strength, and sensing something missing in our own civilization, we take an interest in them as well, and find that they reflect our scientific understanding better than closed systems of faith.

The move towards the esoteric, which emphasizes the inward way and universal consciousness, is taking place at the expense of the exoteric, which emphasizes formal ritual and the distinction between one expression of faith and another. A similar shift of consciousness, in which the politics of coercion and division yields to the politics of inner power and connectedness, has yet to take place. But there is a movement towards it, if only in the widespread disillusionment with conventional structures and ideologies, the distrust of politicians and rejection of their adversarial game. At the same time, there is a new feeling of urgency about the need for change and an understanding that something has gone terribly wrong. These two parallel tendencies both express a desire for a different style of politics, based on different assumptions and reflecting more profound concerns than the petty, largely personal squabbles that the prevailing adversarial mode encourages. Likewise, the desire for change is at the same time a desire for a return to founding principles of freedom, reason and justice – and a movement away from the trivial, materialistic attachments that turn those principles inside out.

A politics of Many-Sidedness is about re-opening the political system, so that it is based on free inquiry and attempts to arrive at truth, rather than polarizing 'debate' and temporary advantage for one faction over another. As such, the distinctions of 'left' and right' become irrelevant, if they ever had any true meaning. What is important is the way in which politicians and movements view their fellow humans (and other beings) and their approach to the search for truth. What matters is whether they place quality before quantity and measure success in more than material terms. As such, Many-Sidedness can be used as a tool by conservatives, who value stability and continuity over unsettling and destabilizing change that takes power away from citizens. But it is of equal use to radicals who wish to examine social problems from the roots upwards. Both are engaged in the same process but starting from different premises. Both are interested in holistic approaches that reach across political and social divisions.

In the same way, there are Many-Sided ideologies at different points on the political compass. They have more in common with each other than their one-sided allies. It is now a truism, except among a few diehards, that fascism and Communism had much in common. In both movements, the individual was seen as subordinate to a collective will and enemies (class in one case, racial in the other) were to be uprooted and destroyed. The two totalitarian systems converged, despite their apparent opposition, because they shared a way of thinking that overrides the differences between them. Human supremacy lay at the heart of both ideologies, with the supremacy of some human groups over others under the direction of an all-powerful state. The result, in both cases, was human and ecological disaster.

In our own time, the prevailing ideology of neo-liberal economics has become a form of free-market fundamentalism, in which individual men and women are defined solely in terms of what they produce and consume, and every aspect of human life, including social solidarity and ties of family and friendship, are seen as subordinate to 'market forces'. A superficial and wholly materialistic idea of 'freedom' is belied by a deterministic approach to the market, in which it creates its own 'adjustments', whatever the social cost or environmental impact.

Like other forms of fundamentalism, this approach is stuck in linear, mechanistic thinking. Its champions on the right believe that market forces unleash enterprise and initiative, and are preferable to costly and unwieldy state control. Some on the left in turn see market forces as agents of opportunity and 'meritocracy'. But real human beings are not the same as the 'actors' in economists' 'models' and need more than material satisfaction, and the spread of market fundamentalism has been accompanied by dramatic rises in violence, addiction, family and community breakdown. By denying the spiritual and social dimension and reducing us to mere economic machines, this form of fundamentalism has dehumanized and denatured us. Any material gains have been offset by a powerful, compelling sense of loss. The cult of 'market forces' separates human beings from each other. At the same time, and for the same reasons, it disrupts our sense of continuity with the environment, making us see it as a series of 'resources' to be controlled and exploited, rather than as a network of ecosystems that sustain life, and of which we are an integral part.

The issue in question is not, as adversarial politics claims, a choice between market and state, individual and community, environment and development. Markets are economically and socially useful, and so is state intervention to redress inequalities and protect vulnerable communities, species or ecosystems. Individual liberty is invaluable, but without social solidarity it is in fact non-existent. No development of any meaningful kind can take place without respect for, and working with, the environment. Although the poorest communities suffer first from pollution and climatic chaos, affluence and privilege provide no shield, any more than they would from the consequences of nuclear war. Human beings of all backgrounds have a vested interest in working with the rest of nature and using their technical skills for just and compassionate purposes. Our ethical evolution must match our scientific and intellectual evolution if our lives are to remain viable.

Therefore we do not need to 'choose' between market and state, or the individual and social aspects of our being. Such choices are counter-productive because they are one-sided, and elevate one area of human experience above all others. In effect, we turn them into false gods. All four areas of human activity are appropriate and valid, as long as they are used with care and not treated as sacrosanct. To elevate one above the other is like poisoning the stomach at the same time as we purify the liver. Society, like the human individual, and like the environment on which we depend, is organic. This is why the aim of politics should not be confrontation, but arriving at a balance between different human needs, within a framework that acknowledges our limits as much as our possibilities and is as wary of our destructive powers as it is welcoming of our creative energy. The political process should be one of unfolding, not of closing doors or the silencing of voices.

More important than the ideological starting point is the attitude that those who enter politics bring to it. One of the main problems with the adversarial approach is that it encourages men and women who enter politics to do so with a conflict-based, confrontational mindset that worsens the longer they remain active. This mindset equates strength with force, power with coercion and suppression, the winning of arguments with the loudest voice, the heaviest fist or – in the worst cases – the most ruthless use of weapons or the cruelest acts of violence.

The adversarial mindset spans the political range. Therefore, it should be no surprise at all when formerly avowed leftists begin to espouse Neoconservative foreign policies that involve the invasion and conquering of non-western countries, with a view to imposing 'western values' as well as safeguarding or expanding western economic interests. The language is the same: that of 'struggle', 'victory', 'culture wars' and 'clash of civilizations'. The mentality is also the same: one in which righteous anger is equated with political strength, rather than seen as an indication of weakness and fear. And so it is in many ways unhelpful to see such changes as ideological shifts at all. They are simply switches from one adversarial stance to another, with an underlying continuity between them – that of one-sidedness.

At another level, some of those who become committed environmentalists or animal rights campaigners display a chilling contempt for their fellow humans, and sometimes a disregard for human life. These activists have not ceased to be human-centered, but have only turned the human-centered approach on its head. In so doing, they are acting out the desires of their (human) egos, which have become more important than the animals or living systems they are claiming to 'protect'. They are also continuing to separate humanity from the rest of nature, viewing the latter as pristine and wholly good, the former as wholly destructive and tainted, with the exception of an elect few. This is essentially the same error as regarding indigenous peoples as 'Noble Savages', that is to say, outsiders or others, rather than full human beings. In denigrating humanity and elevating an external 'nature', such environmental campaigners are not really reconnecting with the natural world because they still see human beings as outside it. Inversion is the opposite of integration.

On the other end of the green spectrum are those environmentalists who deny that human numbers are an issue for us as we rebalance our relationship with the earth. They view 'environmentalism' as a series of structural adjustments, with human behavior remaining largely the same. In this one-sided view of the environment, they avoid challenging a system of values based on human proliferation beyond sustainable numbers, to produce more workers and consumers. This encroaches on other species and threatens our own viability. Living lightly on earth means abandoning the idea that human activity can grow unchecked, without reference to those around us.

Thus belief in 'environmental issues' is no guarantee of political or social openness. It can be just one other one-sided position among many, another example of Ekant. Our relationship with the environment is not, in reality, a series of issues that can be compartmentalized or separated out from the rest of our experience as human beings. It cannot be solved through policy initiatives, or even a radical change of economic direction, unless these arise from a change of consciousness. That change is based on the principle of Careful Action, which is one of the most powerful expressions of Many-Sidedness.

Careful Actions, Careful Thoughts

The idea of Careful Action, in the Jain dharma, is one of the rules imposed on ascetics who have vowed to do no harm to others. It is also, for lay men and women, a practical guide for finding peace with fellow creatures and one's inner self.

Instead of merely demanding the 'right to choose' an action, we need to ask questions of ourselves and each other about that action:

What effect will it have on us?
What effect will it have on others?
What effect will it have on society?
What effect will it have on the planet?
What effect will it have a generation or more from now?

Thus the principle of Careful Action differs both from the short-termism of consumer society and the culture of protest, with its own shopping list of demands and entitlements. It asks us to examine our actions in relation to their impact on others, not just fellow humans, and not only the living but those yet to be born. At one level, it arises from our understanding that our 'self' is but one small unit of life among billions, within a universe too vast for us fully to understand. At another, it allows for an expanded sense of the self, in which we connect it with all other life. There is no contradiction between these two positions, just as there is no contradiction between celebrating human intelligence and being intelligent enough to accept the limits of human knowledge. Far from diminishing us, such understanding gives us the power to reorder our priorities, to adopt a long-range view of our needs, taking account of what we have inherited and what we intend to pass on to future generations. For many indigenous cultures, this is an instinctive response to the dilemmas of living as a human being. This is reflected in the 'Seventh Generation Principle', drawn from the political culture of the Iroquois people. The principle has been adopted by Native American elders and activists, and makes a connection between the rights of Native Americans and their holistic view of the world. Oren Lyons, a chief of the Haudenosaunee (Iroquois) nation, has expressed the principle in this way:

> What about the seventh generation? Where are you taking them? What will they have?

The seventh generation principle applies to the ancestors as well. In honouring the ancestors, one expresses gratitude to them as the seventh generation, which they kept foremost in their decision making and for whom they sacrificed. As a general injunction to live responsibly and respectfully, and as a practical guide to specific moral decision-making, the seventh generation principle may be without equal:

> We say that the faces of coming generations are looking up from the earth. So when you put your feet down, you put them down very carefully – because there are generations coming one after the other. If you think in these terms, then you'll walk a lot more carefully, be more respectful of this earth.[24]

There is even a movement to add a Seventh Generation Amendment to the United States constitution, thus bringing indigenous and imported political philosophies together in a creative fusion. Also known as the Common Property Amendment, its proposed text is:

> The right of citizens of the United States to use and enjoy air, water, wildlife and other renewable resources determined by the Congress to be common property, and shall not be impaired, nor shall such use impair their availability for the

use of future generations.[25]

One of the champions of this Amendment is longstanding Native American campaigner and former vice-presidential candidate Winona LaDuke.[26]

Nonetheless, the concept of a Seventh Generation Amendment, or the simple principle of looking beyond present needs and concerns, is out of step with much of modern democratic politics. This is especially true of an era when politics is dominated by media concerns: instant gratification, instant fame, instant demands and results. Yet the idea of looking beyond the immediate and beyond the self is in tune with our present ecological concerns. Not only does it relate directly to issues such as climate change and pollution, which arise from human impact on nature, in the name of economic expansion, without reference to the environment or future generations. It also points to an alternative model of development, based on respect for the processes of life and on long-term thinking.

Mahatma Gandhi's model for India, *swadeshi*, was based on co-operation, local production for local need and an economics that served the whole of the community, not just centers of affluence and political power. India chose a different form of development, based first on centralized planning, then on free-market economics. This combination has led to economic superpower status, of which Indians are rightly proud, but at the same time to widening and more obvious inequalities, mounting ecological concerns and a sense of spiritual loss. India's experience has become an accelerated version of the western model of 'development' and 'growth'. The same is true for China, where in response to the rise of consumerism and the cult of growth, a government once committed to militant atheism has now launched an inquiry into the spiritual needs of its people and how those might best be fulfilled. Swadeshi, with its emphasis on self-sufficiency, ecology and the local, its stand beyond market and state, is perhaps an idea whose time is come. It is certainly compatible with the principle of Careful Action, and addresses the needs of those who are disenchanted with materialism but value individual liberty, who seek change but want to preserve those traditions that are life-affirming and ensure social stability. Swadeshi is a political economy of Careful Action. By whatever name we choose to call it, it is accessible across the political spectrum and to economies at all stages of development, as the iniquities of expansionist economics become ever more apparent.

The principles of Careful Action originated with Jain ascetics, who practiced it in a literal way to inspire the laity to more virtuous lives. Virtue is not narrowly defined as the observance of social conventions and taboos. Outward appearance is only relevant when it is part of a process of inward transformation. Yet that inner transformation has a direct bearing on the way we behave towards others, human and non-human. It also informs our wider relationship with 'creation' as we still tend to call it in the west, but in Jain terms the continuous cycles of nature and the universe. The shift in personal consciousness and the change in ecological consciousness are parallel processes. As individuals change their lives to reduce their wanton consumption of the earth's resources, so they reduce their level of personal karma. As they unconsciously absorb the influence of previous lives and make choices that liberate their future lives, they help to liberate the planet from harmful influence and ensure the continuity of life on earth.

In this context, the process of 'letting go' is the ultimate act of engagement. When we step back from the materialistic obsessions that rule our lives, we become aware of continuities that link us to past and future generations. For the Jains, this continuity is expressed through samsara, the cycle of birth, death and rebirth, and karma, which carries past-life influences forward and affects our future lives, in whatever form. In dispelling the illusion of separateness and reconnecting with the web of life, we are reducing negative karmic influences. As the *Tattvartha Sutra* cautions:

Sa gupti-samiti-dharma-nupreksa-parisahajaya-caritra [Karmic] inflow is inhibited by guarding [one's actions and protecting life], careful movement, morality, reflection, conquering hardships, and enlightened conduct.

That is the specifically Jain approach to Careful Action, as an enactment of Ahimsa. It is now, especially, an idea that has universal relevance, as we learn to measure the consequences of our actions and realize that even small decisions we make have much wider ramifications. Applied to politics, the principle of Careful Action can give us a sense of proportion, whether we look at things from the radical or conservative point of view. It shows us that ideological divisions are less important than shared human concerns and the way we interact with each other, and just as importantly with fellow creatures. At the same time, it shows us how much our choices matter and that social transformation is not simply a top-down process, but the sum total of many personal transformations.

Careful Action is a spiritual journey for the individual and human society alike. And most important of all, perhaps, it contains the idea of careful thought. The division between thought and actions is one of the artificial distinctions we have learned to make in western culture. In reality, there is no either/or. Thoughts inspire direct physical acts, and they are actions in themselves, because they shape so much of our behavior, affect our physical and mental health, the way we perceive ourselves and others. Many indigenous and pre-literate societies are alive to this, when they blur the distinction between dreams and waking states, accepting that the former might influence the latter. Western psychology has been transformed by our understanding of the unconscious and the profound influence of its workings. Anekant is rooted in a culture that accepts the idea of reincarnation and with it the transfer of thoughts, impressions and experiences from one life, one 'self', to another, with an underlying, consistent true self that is working towards enlightenment. Because rebirth crosses the divisions of species, the experience of the self includes all the cycles of evolution. Ancestor-worshipping cultures, derided as 'primitive' in the 'civilized' west, acknowledge this truth as well, in the idea of continuity within change and a thread of life connecting the generations and overriding the distinction between past, present and future.

Anekant takes these intuitions from the unconscious, or the right side of the brain, and unites them with left-brained reasoning. It therefore has clear implications for the way we construct our thoughts and how we apply them to those around us. Thought control is crucial, but not in the sense that we have come to understand the term, that of controlling other people's thoughts. Instead, we must learn to control our own, in keeping with the practice of self-conquest or the liberation of the true self. Many-Sided thinking is worked towards by breaking through the negative patterns of thought that imprison us. Feelings of hatred, prejudice and self-centered cravings damage our inner selves as much as they damage others. Fanaticism – one-sidedness – limits our own thinking as much as it threatens the freedoms of others. It arises from attachment and becomes an attachment in itself, as potent as material attachment. One-sided thinking leads to the breakdown of communications between human beings, the separation of humanity from nature and a lack of self-awareness. As such it is the root of violence towards the self and others.

Applied to politics, the practice of careful thinking involves constant criticism of one's own beliefs and the motives that underlie them. Far from abandoning principle, this process involves a sharpening of principle by testing one's beliefs against others. Such testing is not confrontational, although we so often confuse confrontation with democratic processes. Instead, it involves the attempt to find common ground with others, including those whose starting points appear profoundly different from our own. Anekant is a journey from many places towards the same destination, and this applies as much to the political as the spiritual journey.

Careful thinking also involves being able to look beyond the short-term material interests promoted by adversarial politics. This is how political thought and the actions that stem from it can be transformed from instruments of conflict into a process of healing. A politics of Many-Sidedness means moving from short-term goals to long-term thinking. It is a movement of transition from narrow individualism to self-awareness, from illusions of exclusivity to a sense of common purpose. The argument against such moves is usually that 'ordinary' people are locked hopelessly into a cycle of consumerism and material attachment. Yet it is the 'political class' of opinion formers and activists who in reality find this transition most difficult. In particular, those who consider themselves progressives fear that abandoning their righteous anger will dilute the cause of social justice. Because they have right on their side, the struggle must continue, whatever the effect on the ideals they espouse and those they claim to represent. Thus many who would seem to be natural supporters of Many-Sidedness become implacable opponents who confuse Careful Action with surrender.

Beyond 'Progressive' and 'Conservative'

He who fights with monsters should look to it that he himself does not become a monster. When you gaze into the abyss, the abyss also gazes into you.
Friedrich Nietzsche

Some weeks after the US-led invasion of Iraq in 2003, and shortly before the cinema-cliché images of toppling statues of dictators, a young activist presented me with a leaflet in London's Russell Square. Ironically, that district of central London would itself be the scene of carnage two years later, in the terrorist outrage of '7/7', which was the direct result of this conflict. The leaflet inveighed against the war and its authors, President George W. Bush and Prime Minister Tony Blair. It claimed to be anti-war and pro-peace, although the latter phrase was not used and the tone was purely negative. Overall, there was something troubling about the leaflet: the predictable, yet still vicious insults, the extreme and florid rhetoric, the invective in place of clear arguments. There was a call for 'resistance', the nature of which was unspecified but implicitly violent. Even the schlock horror background of bloodstains aroused vague unease.

But the leaflet's outstanding feature was its sheer lack of balance. Messrs Blair and Bush were represented as evil incarnate. Meanwhile, Iraqi dictator Saddam Hussein escaped the mildest criticism, let alone reference to the widespread torture and murder of political opponents, or the use of poisoned gas against the Kurdish and Marsh Arab minorities. When I put some of these questions to the anti-war activist, he replied that violence was not the issue, merely 'the context of the violence'. Nor was peace really the issue, but 'opposition to capitalism and war'. He was explicit, and laudably honest, about his true political objectives, his belief in violent change and in peace marches as a means (one of many) towards that end. Like President Bush, he believed that 'either you're with us or against us'. It was only the 'us' that differed.

At roughly the same time, an art historian whose work I was editing described to me the discrimination she had faced within her discipline. This discrimination was directed at her principally as a woman, but also as a political exile from Eastern Europe living in London. She was, it seemed, still smoldering inwardly from the patronizing put-downs and rudeness she had experienced in the 1970s. 'If you don't always struggle, how do you win victories?' she demanded, in an unconscious echo of the Communist regime she had escaped. At that moment, her combative expression suddenly fell and was replaced by a look of profound unhappiness, even despair. Far from celebrating (as she most certainly deserved to do) her success in rising above petty prejudice, she admitted that she was still eaten up with anger. Her urge to struggle had taken over her emotional and intellectual life to the extent that no success could placate her and no 'victory' could ever be final enough. She had not risen above the prejudice, for it consumed her like a cancer of the soul.

These two examples illustrate two serious problems with the way we think about and organize politics. The first of these is the way in which the adversarial approach has taken over political discourse and governs virtually every aspect of it. Human sympathy and tolerance give way to dogmatic certainties, and moralistic slogans veil amoral and cynical acts. 'Winning' becomes an absolute principle, an end in itself, overriding any attempt to arrive at truth. Captivated by the 'struggle' for 'victory', politicians and activists ignore the detrimental effects of one-sided thinking on victors and vanquished alike. They ignore the corruption of the ideal being 'struggled' for and the way it becomes toxic and contaminated with hatred.

The second and closely related problem is with movements that style themselves as progressive, be they political parties or single-issue campaigns. Inspired by worthwhile goals of social justice, equality and non-discrimination, and seeking positive change, they often take on the most negative aspects of their adversaries, usually those characteristics they most fervently oppose. The bellicose peace protester, the feminist who is hostile and demeaning towards men (and women who disagree with her) and the animal rights campaigner who is indifferent and callous towards humans might all be seen as stereotypes. Yet they pervade the political landscape, and all of us have met them, listened to them, read their articles, or been affected by their actions in some way.

These progressive campaigners have their reactionary counterparts. There is the anti-abortionist who is pro-life but supports the death penalty. There is the family values campaigner who is indifferent to child poverty. Or, in the British context, there is the 'Euro-skeptic' who opposes the growing influence of the European Union over national sovereignty, but adopts an attitude of submissiveness towards US foreign policy or the wishes of trans-national corporations. These are examples of ways in which adversarial politics encourage stereotypical thinking and cardboard cut-out policy stances. By its very nature, this way of 'doing' politics stifles creative thought and shuts off both intellectual and practical possibilities.

In their fervent embrace of adversarialism, progressive movements and their members suffer at two levels. First, they are co-opted: they are changed by the adversarial system, rather than transforming it as they had once hoped. Secondly, they lose their positive energy, the reason for their existence in the first place, and replace it with anger, fanaticism and personality cults. The more angry and fanatical a progressive movement becomes, the less likely it is to challenge the status quo. This is because its members lose their sense of proportion, and perspective. They become convinced that the opinions they have reached are beyond challenge, even by those on whose behalf they act. Their opinions have become attachments and possessions rather than instruments in a search for truth.

To be true to our principles, therefore, we need to be able to stand back from them and realize that we do not have a monopolistic, exclusive view of the truth. Living out our principles does not mean adopting an attitude of perpetual opposition and anger. For that, in reality, is to lose our direction and to lose our creative power. Creative use of principle involves finding common ground, whatever our starting point, in placing compassion for fellow humans and creatures before the consumption and economic expansion that do violence against the earth and ourselves. The search for truth involves conserving ecological and cultural diversity, and progressing beyond our limited understanding of progress, in which we equate it with material attachment and separation from nature. A politics of Many-Sidedness starts with a holistic balancing of the conserving and progressive impulses within humanity.

Rather than abandoning principle, Many-Sidedness is the refinement or fine-tuning of principle. Working for a more just society and more balanced relations between humanity and nature is not merely an option, but part of the quest for truth that is the basis of Many-Sided thinking. Many-Sidedness means realizing that our ideas do not automatically give us superior knowledge and that they lose their real power when we close our minds to other possibilities.

The ancient Indian technique of Anekant, passed down by the Jains, is a gift for all of humanity. It is a guide for us as we adapt to a more closely connected, interdependent world. In learning to live within limits, we fulfill our potential. In constant questioning of ourselves, we achieve true power.

Notes

1 From Barbara C. Sproul, *Primal Myths* (San Francisco: Harper & Row, 1979), pp.192-4. See also www.aboutastronomy.com/topics/Jinasena

2 See www.fas.harvard.edu/~pluralism/affiliates/jainism/quite/greatment.htm

3 K.V. Mardia, *The Scientific Foundations of Jainism* (Delhi: Motilal Banarsidass, 2002), pp.4-5

4 www.shambhuskitchen.co.uk

5 Hugletts Wood Farm, Grovelye Lane, Dallington, East Sussex TN21 9PA, United Kingdom

6 *Resurgence* magazine, Ford House, Hartland, Bideford, Devon EX39 6EE, UK
Tel. ++44 (0)1237 441293. www.resurgence.org

7 www.meghraj.com

8 The surname Shah is frequent among Jains of Gujarati origin. It is not derived from the Farsi word for king (as is sometimes claimed), but related to the Gujurati word 'sah' (businessman) and the word 'sadhu', meaning honest or good, and also gentleman or monk.

9 Diverse Ethics Ltd, 9 Redmill, Colchester CO3 4RT, UK. Tel. ++44 (0)78 042 94903. www.diverseethics.com
Email: atul@diverseethics.com

10 Quotations from the *Acaranga Sutra* in this book are taken from the translation by the German Indologists Hermann Jacobi and F. Max Mueller, English versions of which were published in 1882 and 1895.

11 Umasvati, *That Which Is: Tattvartha Sutra*, (San Francisco: Harper Collins, 1994). Introduction by L.M. Singvi, former Indian High Commissioner to the UK, and editing and commentary by Nathmal Tatia. There is also a version of the

Tattvartha Sutra published by Motilal Banarsidass (Delhi) in 2006.

[12] James Gleick, *Chaos: The Making of a New Science* (New York: Viking Penguin, 1987), p.7

[13] Mardia, op. cit., p.13

[14] Bill Devall, *Simple in Means, Rich in Ends: Deep Ecology in Theory and Practice* (London: Green Print, 1990), p.39

[15] ibid., p.40

[16] See Devall, op.cit., pp.38–73, 'The Ecological Self'.

[17] Mardia, op.cit., p.7

[18] George Sessions (ed.), *Deep Ecology for the Twenty-First Century: Readings on the Philosophy and Practice of the New Environmentalism* (Boston & London: Shambhala, 1995), p.68

[19] ibid, pp.64-85

[20] An *Arhat* in Jainism (also *Arihant* or *Arihanta*) is one who has overcome his or her negative impulses and attachments and so achieved self-realisation. It is essentially a synonym for Jina. The meaning of the title is 'destroyer of enemies', the enemies in question being destructive karmas.

[21] Robert Lawlor, *Awakening in the Aboriginal Dreamtime* (Rochester, Vermont: Inner Traditions, 1991), p.70

[22] 'Bushmen' is an umbrella term for a range of southern African hunter-gatherer peoples who have been variously classified as 'Basarwa', 'Khwe', 'Sho', 'San' and other titles. 'Bushman' cultures tend to refer to themselves by the names of individual groups, such as the !Kung, rather than using a generalized term. The word 'Bushman' is placed in inverted commas because, although old-fashioned sounding, it is widely understood and relatively uncontroversial.

[23] See in particular Jean-Jacques Rousseau, *Discourse on the Origins of Inequality* [written in 1755] (Oxford: Oxford University Press (Oxford , New Edition 1999).

[24] See address by Haudenosaunee Faithkeeper Chief Oren Lyons to the United Nations General Assembly, New York City, 10

December 1992: www.thepeoplespaths.net/political/orenl
.htm

Also Sustainable Oregon Schools Initiative. http://sustain
ableschools.org/discover/discover.htm

25 See www.protecttheearth.org

26 Winona LaDuke, *All Our Relations: Native Struggles for Land and Life* (Cambridge, Massachusetts: South End Press, 1999). Winona LaDuke was Ralph Nader's running mate, endorsed by the United States Green Party, in 1996 and 2000. In the elections of 2008, she endorsed Democratic candidate Barack Obama.

Index

B O O K S

O is a symbol of the world, of oneness and unity. In different cultures it also means the "eye," symbolizing knowledge and insight. We aim to publish books that are accessible, constructive and that challenge accepted opinion, both that of academia and the "moral majority."

Our books are available in all good English language bookstores worldwide. If you don't see the book on the shelves ask the bookstore to order it for you, quoting the ISBN number and title. Alternatively you can order online (all major online retail sites carry our titles) or contact the distributor in the relevant country, listed on the copyright page.

See our website **www.o-books.net** for a full list of over 500 titles, growing by 100 a year.

And tune in to myspiritradio.com for our book review radio show, hosted by June-Elleni Laine, where you can listen to the authors discussing their books.

mySpiritRadio